KELLY ASHFORD

endurance

Extreme Survival in the Colorado Rocky Mountain Wilderness

High Desert Publishig

endurance
Extreme Survival in the Colorado Rocky Mountain Wilderness
One Woman's Experience of Near Death, Resilience and Survival
© 2024 Kelly Ashford.

Published by High Desert Publishing

Development Editor: Judith Briles, TheBookShepherd.com
Proofreader: Peggie Ireland
Cover and Interior Design: Rebecca Finkel, F + P Graphic Design, FPGD.com

Books may be purchased in quantity by contacting the publisher through the author's website: KellyAshford.com

Library of Congress Control Number: data on file
ISBN trade paper: 979-8-9896867-2-8
ISBN eBook: 979-8-9896867-1-1
ISBN audiobook: 979-8-9896867-0-4

Survival | Hiking | Memoir | Spirituality

First Edition
Printed in the USA

Dedicated to my husband Thomas,
daughter Paige and son, Ryan
with gratitude for their love and support
throughout my years of recovery
and writing of Endurance.

And to our 'boxer boy's'
Bob and Boomer
and our rescue dogs
Sim and Tula Sue.

They were all my inspiration
to never give up.

Contents

Author's Note vii

one The Game 1

two Seek.. 5

three Forward I Go....................................... 9

four Listen.. 15

five The Energy Within............................... 19

six Security Blanket................................. 25

seven Again, I Ask ... Why? 29

eight Family Memories Are My Companions 33

nine To Fear the Unknown........................... 41

ten Homesick 43

eleven Memories of Mom 49

twelve Thomas ... My Rock........................... 57

thirteen Native Roots.................................... 61

fourteen A Strange Encounter........................... 71

fifteen Trapped by the Storm 77

sixteen Reflection ... Grandma and Grandpa....... 87

seventeen Sacred Places.................................... 91

eighteen My Cornerstones............................... 95

nineteen Lifesaving Trivia............................... 101

twenty Leaving My Shelter 109

twenty-one The Unseen Forest 115

twenty-two The Promise 121

twenty-three Taken Away..................................... 129

twenty-four The Light................................... 133

twenty-five Across the Abyss 139

twenty-six The Shaman's Call............................ 147

twenty-seven The Magical Forest........................... 151

twenty-eight Severe Frostbite................................ 159

twenty-nine My Log Coffin.................................. 165

thirty The River... 171

thirty-one Stroke of Luck.................................. 175

thirty-two Four-Legged Angel 183

thirty-three Rescued!... 191

thirty-four Reunited... 195

thirty-five The Best News 199

thirty-six Forever Changed 207

thirty-seven Fear of the Unknown......................... 211

thirty-eight The Secret Continues......................... 221

thirty-nine Where Am I Headed?......................... 225

forty Hand of God 233

forty-one Home at Last................................. 241

forty-two My Final Thoughts........................... 245

Epilogue.. 249

Meet Kelly Ashford... 253

How to Work with Kelly Ashford 254

Acknowledgments... 255

List of Supplies for a Day Hike............................. 257

 # Author's Note

Have you ever been brought to your knees, desperate to survive, and questioned your real purpose in life?

That's where I was in June of 2010. Lost. Hallucinating. Starving. Terrified.

This was the time in my life that had the ability to forever change the way I understand and perceive my life's purpose. For some, such a significant life event can be simply *interesting*. For others it's a *wake-up* call, something profound and difficult to describe. Or it may be a *profound spiritual awakening*, forever altering your life.

For me, it was and is all three … and more. I spent eleven days … terrifying days in the Rocky Mountain wilderness that ended with my rescue laying by the Williams Fork River. I felt I was dying over and over. That I had been pulled into hell. That my life was over.

As you read *Endurance*, you will encounter the interesting, the wake-up calls, and the profound spiritual awakening. My life that June became a series of unfortunate ordeals that felt like they were never-ending: in my mind; in my body; in my soul.

This is my story, all true … eleven days that changed my life … and my husband's … and my children's.

No matter how I processed my experience, the short- and long-term of it, I now understand it requires me to *choose the lesson*, to consciously signify the moment and internalize the information, the lesson, the calling … the message to me.

one
The Game

Gratefully, the Voice and the Game have departed ...

I don't remember exactly when "it" first intruded into my life. There was never an invitation: not by email, a phone call, or over coffee. But I was poked.

When did it start?

I remember a voice talking to me. It was a male voice flooding me with information, directions, places to go ... even numbers. It made no sense to me. Why was it contacting me?

I remember times when I was in my car ... a car I affectionately called Hazel ... and it, and I, would go into automatic. As in being a driverless car, it was taking over as if it didn't need me: the human operator.

Almost hypnotizing as I think back, it was misdirecting me when I had a destination planned, and telling me I had to buy something, then telling me I had to discard something—always in a clear and persistent manner.

In 2005, lupus autoimmune disease grabbed ahold of my life. My ability to provide a livelihood was cut off. It changed me in a profound way and my quest for natural healing began.

When did it start? A "Voice" took me over and then there was "the Game."

It started when we moved into a rental house in 2008. Thomas and I have come to think of it as the bad rental seed when we got caught like millions of others in the collapsing mortgage markets. Our home became an upside-down nightmare to hold on to, so we had no choice but to let it go. We became renters until we could buy once again.

Weirdness became the new normal around us.

Weird things were happening.

With the kids.

With the kids' friends when they visited and when they left the house.

With items in the house.

With our dogs.

With us.

With Thomas.

With me.

As I write this, thirteen years have passed. I continue to heal from the trauma that I endured. It has been extensive, introducing PTSD to my life and everyday living. My faith and prayers were integral parts in my coping and making me whole once again. Daily I recited and prayed with a lengthy exorcism prayer. Today, I use a shorter version, a prayer to Saint Michael.

The Voice continued for a few years: encouraging me to take chances; to drive places, to take risks. Sometimes it was able to lure me, pulling me back into the Game.

Through faith, prayer, and energy healing, I have come back stronger than ever in my conviction of Jesus Christ and all the blessings that lay ahead in my life, my family's, and that of humanity. The experience of being lost in the wilderness was terrifying. It took many years to recover from the ordeal, but it also gave me a connection to nature and wildlife and a spiritual renewal that I never had before. Since then, spending time in the mountains and outdoors always brings a time of restoration, gratitude, and awe at God's splendor.

Gratefully, the Voice and the Game have departed … most likely to bait and hook another. My faith, my prayers, and my family saved me from what was to become my extreme survival in the Colorado Rocky Mountain wilderness.

two
Seek ...

Good and not-so-good thoughts
boomeranged in my mind.

I left the house in the early morning in my typical summer attire—shorts, T-shirt, and flip-flops—and hopped into Hazel, my Nissan Pathfinder. It was an unseasonably warm spring day driving around downtown Denver, circling the capitol, driving to places I had lived growing up, bringing up childhood memories. I was in a nostalgic, meditative mood, And the warmth of the day relaxed me. It was June 8, 2010.

Seeking clues from the past to shed light on understanding myself and the person I had grown to be was the driving force behind my wandering and reflecting. Good and not-so-good thoughts boomeranged in my mind—about me and others in my life.

I knew in my heart that I was a kind, generous, and loving person with compassion for others. I also had a side that was not so virtuous that I struggled to come to terms with. My thoughts that morning were of wanting to surround myself with peace and calm.

I drove to a childhood home where I had lived for about five years. The neighborhood still looked the same; poor, but more run-down than I remembered with just a few well-cared-for homes here and there.

Stopping, I parked Hazel but remained in the car. I studied the house built in 1949 in southwest Denver. I think homes absorb the energy of people that live in them, and my former home appeared desolate and unkempt. Smaller than I remembered, it needed paint on its concrete slab walls. The grounds were scrubby and barren. Dirt was the primary landscape feature.

It had been my refuge from the chaos at home.

The porch that my six-foot-six stepdad threw my five-foot-one mother off of was about two feet high. My childhood impression was that it was much higher, but back then I was just a small kid, maybe five years old.

That memory had been seared into my mind by the fear I had felt at seeing my mom collapsed and crying loudly with pain as she lay in the yard unable to walk. The bones in her foot were shattered, crushed by the fall. Already crippled by polio, her bad foot was now mangled and would require surgery to put it back together.

As I sat in the car, I focused on the porch and relived the memory, remembering the violence and shock. It was not a happy house then, nor did it appear to be a happy, cared-for home now. What were the happy times way back … if any?

Some. There were times of laughter and fun in our household.

A huge truck tire swing was tied high into one of the trees along a creek that we played on in the summer. In the winter, we sledded down the creek embankment, sometimes sliding onto the frozen creek and breaking through the ice. The swinging and sledding were the only times I recall laughter and freedom in our house.

The small creek that ran to the right of the house and across the street was now encased by concrete walls. The large trees and vegetation that I remembered playing in were gone. It had been my refuge from the chaos at home.

I was a tomboy at heart and enjoyed being outside. I had spent many pleasant hours playing in the creek. Barefoot, wading in the water and building mud dams, catching crawdads, studying plant life, watching mudskippers and little fish were the escape that my brothers and sisters and I had from the torment within our walls.

Trying to focus on the good times, I remembered the endless hours we spent playing games of tag and hide-and-seek outdoors. We had so much fun and found happiness in the simple things. Yes, there were a few positives.

These were the bonding times with my siblings—two stepbrothers and one stepsister, along with my older brother and sister.

Ours was a blended family of six children for the ten years Mom was married to our stepdad. We were one big dysfunctional family, with ages ranging from three to nine years old.

I needed clarity and calm.

It was all so long ago. I am now 45 years old, a mother of two children that I love with all my heart but am still looking for direction.

Coming here did not provide answers or closure that I was seeking. I needed clarity and calm. The answer was in front of me, two hours away. Almost having a mind of her own, Hazel headed to the mountains.

And I ... why was I along? I could only assume it was to meditate, to seek out alone time to clear my head and heal in nature.

Or was it something else?

three
Forward I Go …

June 9, 2010 | **DAY ONE**

It was as though Hazel was in charge as we drove through Boulder and then Lyons with my hands on her steering wheel, as her chassis headed toward Estes Park.

My children were my biggest joy and I loved being their mother. All I ever wanted was their happiness by providing a safe, stable, and loving homelife. But life had not worked out as I had hoped or planned, and my children had been through some difficult times. My sorrow was immense. I felt like I had failed them when my marriage to their father fell apart.

Snow Mountain Ranch was just a few miles outside of Estes Park. A sweet memory of camping there with my daughter, Paige, and my son, Ryan, on a Girl Scout trip entered my mind and I felt a smile cross my face. We had some great times there … long ago.

I really needed to ground myself, get my head out of the past, and try to get control back in my life, I thought. I wanted to take this time to meditate and recall all that I was grateful for: my children; Thomas, my soulmate, best friend, and husband for the last eight years; and my large extended family. I was blessed in many ways and had much to be grateful for.

Estes Park is one of my favorite places. As I entered its main street, officially labeled as N St Vrain Street, I drove slowly so I could look at the many quaint shops that were popular with tourists. It was such a cute little town, and a hugely popular spot because of its location at the base of the entrance to Rocky Mountain National Park.

Looping back to the main road, I entered the park and drove up to the small shack where the park ranger was taking money from the park visitors.

At the ranger's window I read that the entrance fee is waived if you are on disability. I had my proof of disability with me and handed it to the guard, along with my driver's license. He gave me a newly printed National Parks Disability Pass and returned my disability paper and license. I was grateful for the free admission. A twenty-dollar bill was all I had on me.

Thanking the guard, I entered the park to soak up the beauty of my surroundings. Pulling over to the side of the road, I scanned the Visitor Information Guide the ranger had given me and learned a brief history of the park.

Its beginning was marked with the arrival of the Paleo-Indians when they traveled along what is now Trail Ridge Road to hunt and forage for food. They were followed by the Ute and Arapaho people who hunted and camped in the area. Settlers began arriving in the mid-1800s. Eventually, many of the Native Americans left the area by 1860. Within twenty years, those who hadn't left were removed to reservations.

The park was stunning. It includes the Rocky Mountains, alpine lakes, and a wide variety of wildlife within various climates and environments—climates and environments changeable in mere minutes. Wooded forests of aspen, ponderosa pine, high elevation willow, spruce, and fir were part of the mountain tundra.

It was home to a variety of wildlife ... from the many predatory animals, including Canada lynx, foxes, bobcat, cougar, black bear, and coyotes, along with deer, marmot, moose, and hundreds of species of birds. For me, it's a nature lover's dream to be able to access it so easily.

It can get cold here during the winter months ... as in Arctic conditions that can hit –35 degrees Fahrenheit or below. Headline-making blizzards, high winds, and deep snow are prevalent during the winter months.

The park was a treat and a visit to "God's country." The mountains were majestic and called to me with their resplendent beauty. I steered the car back onto Highway 34 that turned into Trail Ridge Road and wound around through the park.

The endless stream of cars filled with tourists drove slowly through the park. Most tourists fell in love with Colorado when they visited here—four million people yearly.

Few realize how high in elevation the road gradually climbed and suddenly the magnificent top appears. The views were stunning. High atop the mountain peak, Trail Ridge Road was the fourth highest paved road in the United States. It is known as the "highway to the sky," crossing the Continental Divide at 12,183 feet elevation.

The drop-off on the side of the road was insanely steep but a phenomenally spectacular place to view from. It's also an OMG, white-knuckle ride if you are afraid of heights. One wrong move on the very narrow two-lane road could mean death.

I was near that highest point in the road when almost of its own accord, the steering wheel pulled to the left and I found myself at the Ute trailhead parking lot.

Hazel, why are we here? I thought.

There were a few other cars parked at the overlook. People were sitting on rocks looking out at the spectacular vista below. One could see for miles and miles on this clear, beautiful June day.

Stepping out of the car, it wasn't as warm as I thought it was. I immediately shivered in the sharp, cold wind and pulled on a long-sleeved T-shirt and windbreaker over my short-sleeve tee. I was not prepared for the high-altitude weather, dressed in a pair of gym shorts and flip-flops. Although the skies were clear blue, it was bone-chilling cold. The afternoon sun offered little warmth.

Feeling compelled to get out and walk, I put on a pair of socks, knowing I could not walk on the steep trail in my flip-flops. I was only going a little way … just far enough to be alone, find a nice spot to sit, pray, and read the Gideon's Bible that I had brought along.

At least, that was my intention.

Before I started down the trail, I stopped to admire the spectacular vistas and chatted with a couple of tourists from Russia who commented on the beautiful views. They were very friendly and said they really loved being in the USA. I welcomed them to Colorado and said I was happy they were enjoying their trip. Wishing them safe travels, I bid them goodbye.

As I headed down the trail, an Asian man said to me, "Are you sure you should be going? You may not be dressed for it," as he looked down at my feet in socks, without shoes.

I cheerily replied, "I'm only going a short distance. I'll be okay."

"The Beaver Trail is hard to find. Are you sure?"

"I am … thanks!" Giving him a quick wave, I continued on my way. But I thought it was nice that he was concerned about my welfare.

Why wasn't I?

His words turned out to be quite prophetic of my coming demise.

four
Listen ...

Why has the Voice compelled me to continue?

Above the tree line was the Ute Trail, a narrow and steep dirt path. Before setting out, I did a series of circles, twirls, not really knowing why. What was that about? I was not thinking on my own; the Voice was still there, guiding me, filling my body.

Go forward, Kelly, the mountain awaits you.

Forward I went. It was mostly rocky and dry soil, dusty, due to the elevation of 11,430 feet, which was above the tree line. The temperature was bitterly cold and my legs felt it. I needed to get moving to warm them up. As I walked about three-quarters of a mile down the mountain, the trail now wove among pine trees and other plants and shrubs.

I left the car around 3:00 p.m. Although I was going very slowly downhill, my stocking feet were starting to feel cold, wet, and bruised. I stopped abruptly, realizing that I was caught up in my thoughts, distracted, and had lost the trail. I was now walking in snow and my feet were freezing.

Why am I here? Why am I doing this? Is there something I'm supposed to be learning?

There were paint splatters that were fluorescent white on the path. I assumed it was from the maintenance truck I had driven behind because it had been spilling drips of stuff everywhere. But the splatters presented as if they were a guide for me to follow.

Being stubborn, I had it in my mind to get to the Beaver ponds. It had been planted in my head when the man I had encountered walking down the path asked me if I was headed to them. I wasn't then … yet I was now.

In the shady spots, the snow was deep. A feeling of foreboding set in as each foot stepped into the icy-cold snow. It had taken me all afternoon to hike down the mountain and dusk was approaching. I turned back the way I came. I did not feel so adventurous or brave anymore as night fell and my world turned dark.

The stars shone in the sky—brilliant, like tiny diamonds. It was amazing how many were visible without the interference of city lights … so many millions of shining bright lights. It took my breath away when I looked up at the sky and remembered the vastness of the universe. The moon was a quarter crescent as it began its ascent in the sky.

Unable to see in the darkness, I stumbled and fell, again and again, falling over rocks and tree branches that scraped my arms and legs. My left eye had been poked with a tree branch, and it was stinging and blurry. Determined to make it back to my car, I picked myself up over and over again.

Blinded by the darkness, I headed back up the mountain when the sky opened and started to rain lightly and then pour down.

My feet were burning with cold. Never had I been this cold before. My heart was racing. It felt like it was pounding in my throat.

Snow, OMG, it's snowing now.

But then I kept hearing the Voice telling me: *You are meant to be here. You will be okay.*

Being Colorado, the snowstorm passed quickly. The night sky was clear again with its star roommates. I decided to follow the crescent moon as it traveled west in the sky. I knew I had hiked from the west and had headed east. So now I would try to retrace my steps.

As I climbed to higher ground, another rainstorm poured down icy water. I was drenched; there was nothing warm on me. Taking shelter under a tree blocked some of the downpour. And I tied the windbreaker to tree branches to cover my head as a makeshift umbrella to keep the rain and snow off.

The Gideon's Bible I had carried since I left the car was still in my hand. Now soaked through, I placed it next to the tree trunk. I was lost, sitting on the side of a mountain, and no one knew where I was. And in early June, the low temp here on this mountain will go below freezing.

Here I was, sitting under a tree on the soaked ground. Taking off my socks, I held my feet … ice-cold, wet, and burning from the harsh exposure. I stayed awake all night, sitting, hugging my knees, and holding my feet in my icy hands. Saying I was miserable didn't even describe how bad I felt. I felt foolish and angry at myself that I was so ill-equipped for a hike. But most of all, I did not understand why the Voice brought me here. Tears rolled down my face as snow and rain took turns during the night.

Why has the Voice compelled me to continue? Why was I led here?

The night passed. Eventually the snow stopped. I stayed sitting in water running down the mountain, streamlets of water everywhere. I prayed to Jesus, to God, for help from angels and begged to get off this mountain safely and back home.

It was all I wanted to do.

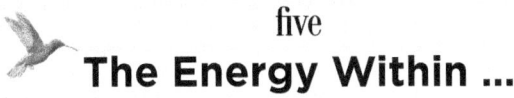

five

The Energy Within ...

Why was I here?

It was a time of reflection of the events that led me here …
now … at this moment. Some were life-changing events and
others were everyday events … normal routines after waking up.
Whatever they were, they brought me to this point in my life.

The summer of 2008, my Uncle Arnold and his wife, Bea, had
flown into town to join my Aunt Vera and Uncle Al's anniversary
dinner party. I enjoyed visiting with them. Bea was a sweet, kind
woman who had brought much love and happiness to Uncle
Arnold, and vice versa. They were one of those couples that seemed
to truly like and love each other.

It was no secret that I was going through a divorce. The whole
family knew, even those I never talked to about it. Out of concern,
Bea asked how I was feeling, health-wise. I was tired and stressed
out, battling autoimmune issues. It was nice to share my feelings
with someone who truly cared. I brought her up to date on the
latest happenings in my life, including lupus, which had become
an uninvited daily guest.

I felt a sense of comfort and peace.

Bea asked if I had heard of Reiki/Energy
Healing. I had not. But I was interested in anything that could
help me self-heal. I didn't know that she was a Reiki Master. She

offered to give me a healing, explaining it would be easier to experience a session, and then talk about it after we were finished.

I was game and laid back on the couch, and she went to work with magic in her hands. As she placed her hands on my shoulders, I felt a sense of comfort and peace. I was immensely grateful for her kindness and her hands that generated warmth as she touched me.

As she placed her hands on different parts of my body, starting at the top of my head and working down to my feet, her hands became very hot. "Your energy is blocked, Kelly. Your body is like a concrete block, filled with stagnant, stuck energy. There is major blockage on your back and shoulders." When I heard her words, I wasn't surprised. I was always feeling stress and tightness there.

I had no knowledge of energy healing, but what Bea told me did not sound good. I was very aware of my chronic fatigue and constant pain. When she finished, I felt calm, at peace … even hopeful. If Bea was a part of this Reiki treatment, I had faith that it would be okay. Just maybe this would be the help I had been searching for. I knew I needed something. The medication prescribed certainly did not deal with the pain levels I was experiencing. There had to be another way.

Bea shared her own personal challenges that she had overcome in her life and what brought her to become a Reiki Healer. She explained that this practice was available to me and, really, for anyone to learn and do self-healing. With much gratitude and a promise to stay in touch, I made a commitment. I told her I wanted to learn to do this for myself, and even be able to help my family, some of whom were suffering from stress and various illnesses.

I was open-minded to alternative methods of healing, having already tried daily handfuls of vitamins and supplements. I followed dietary restrictions, mixes of herbs, and blood purification where I was hooked up to an IV and my blood was cleansed in peroxide. Yes, I was highly motivated to feel better. And I was desperate.

Most days, it was all I could do to merely perform daily tasks. I had been diagnosed with an autoimmune disorder and had a brief stay in the hospital to dissolve blood clots in my dominant hand. I was in dire need of a miracle. My doctors had told me that I was lucky to be alive. Fortunately, I had found a good rheumatologist. Dr. Stuart Kassan was kind, supportive and helped me manage the symptoms of my disease. His patients loved him, and many would travel for hours to see him.

After a nighttime winter hike in Evergreen, Colorado, with Thomas, we stopped at Little Bear, a popular restaurant/bar and ordered a burger and beer. I noticed my fingers were discolored—dark purplish—on my dominant hand. It had been a cold, snowy hike but we had not been outside long enough for me to have frostbite. I kept glancing at my hand, hoping whatever the problem was that it would just go away.

It did not. A few days went by, and my hand was worse. My fingers were turning dark purplish/black. The skin on my fingertips was beginning to peel, like a heel in need of a pedicure. The dead skin was sloughing off.

I made an appointment with my primary doctor. After a brief exam and a few questions, she said I needed to go to the hospital immediately and be admitted for tests. She suspected blood clots. I was admitted to St. Luke's Hospital and an arterial angiography test was performed. A scope was inserted into my groin and a dye injected to take X-rays of the blood vessels in my extremities.

The doctors were surprised to see me, a young woman, with blood clots in fingers, hands, and feet. I was informed that I would be placed in intensive care, and they would treat me with an anticoagulant. There was the potential the injection would dislodge a clot that could go to my brain or lung, and I would die. I signed the release form, scared that I would never see my children or Thomas again.

Nitroglycerine was rubbed into my hand and the treatment began. The other possible outcome was that my fingers and hand would auto-amputate—the flesh would just die and fall off. Thankfully, the clots dissolved and I survived. My hands and fingers were okay. My circulation would never be the same, but they saved my hand. Placed on blood thinners, it became a weekly regimen of blood-draws to monitor my daily medicine.

Remembering the trauma and the drama of the blood clot experience, Bea's words planted the seed. I would find a local Reiki Healer.

I searched on the internet: "Reiki, near me." My destiny continued to unfold. I found a Master Reiki teacher who taught Reiki classes at a hotel just a few blocks from where I lived. I enrolled in a First- and Second-Degree Reiki Training and Certification. It was a weekend class, Friday through Sunday.

I had my first attunement session on a Friday. Lisa was my guide and teacher. She had a positive energy and a gentle, calming presence about her.

I have always loved learning. With the Reiki symbols and their meanings, I absorbed how to channel the energy through meditation and prayer and where to position my hands on the body. During the session, I noticed a tingling sensation in my palms. I could not wait to get home and practice. The palms of my hands were pulsating with energy. I was amazed as the sensation grew stronger. I was looking forward to learning more about this mysterious practice of Reiki. The next day couldn't arrive soon enough.

The next day couldn't arrive soon enough.

Not surprisingly, others in the class felt the palms of their hands tingling with energy, too. Some mentioned seeing colors and had visual impressions. A few felt like they had a cold. This was all normal and part of the healing and cleansing process that the attunement generates.

The first and second levels of Reiki focus on physical and emotional healing. I was already looking forward to learning the Master level of Reiki that incorporates spiritual healing.

Since Bea spoke to me and I attended the Reiki training, my life had changed. I spent hours self-healing. Old memories, trauma, and sadness were brought to the surface and many times I cried ... weeping and remembering. As I healed and moved the energy through my body, I felt lighter. My heavy load of illness and depression started to lift.

As I was cleansing myself of stuck energy, I heard the Voice repeating in my mind: *Sins of the Fathers*. What could that mean? I didn't know, but the message stayed with me.

Why was I here?

Now, isolated that first night in the wilderness, I thought about my children. At this time, Paige was twenty years old and Ryan was eighteen. I might not see them again. The fear became a physical pain. I felt my heart ache and started to cry. I loved them so deeply and did not want them to suffer in any way. I felt like I had failed them. They needed me, and I doubted I would find my way back to the car. And Thomas … he needed me as well, as I needed him. I told myself that I had to quit the "pitiful me" thinking. I had to figure out *why* I was compelled to be here.

I thought about the national park's guide I had read earlier. It was inspiring to know Native Americans had followed this trail on foot. They were brave, with tenacity and spirit to survive, hunting and living off the land. It was sad that they had been forced off of their ancestral land. I could feel their spirits here on this mountain. And it gave me comfort and courage to overcome my fears. I imagined the life they lived certainly had been fraught with danger, mostly from the elements and wildlife. Not too many years ago wolves and grizzlies lived in the area.

Since I had become a Reiki Healer this past year, strange things had been happening to me. The attunement had opened a channel within me to connect to higher wisdom, although it appeared my present predicament was far from wise. I had finished my master's training just a month earlier.

I just hoped I would make it through the night.

six

Security Blanket ...

*My feet burned—icy-cold, shooting pain—
with each step I took.*

June 10, 2010 | **DAY TWO – Ute Trail**

Finally, dawn arrived. As soon as I was able to see in the morning's first light, I pushed myself to standing, wincing at the pain in my wet stocking-clad feet. I knew I was suffering from hypothermia. My feet and hands ached and felt frozen. I walked about a quarter mile down the hill I had crawled up the night before. Slowly and carefully placing each foot on the ground, I made it to the bottom of the ravine.

I felt the fear leave my body in a heavy sigh of relief when I found the Ute Trail leading up to the overlook and my car. Knowing that Hazel was there and waiting for me reseeded my momentum to keep going. I could not believe my good fortune and thanked God and the spirits on the mountain. My feet burned—icy-cold, shooting pain—with each step I took.

It felt like there was an evil presence in the wind.

Walking lightly, it took painstaking time to land each footstep gently on the ground. The beginning of frostbite was making its presence known.

I knew it was about a mile back to the parking lot, straight up. As I hiked up the mountain, the wind was blowing so strong and fierce that I had to crouch over, and at times, put my hands on the ground to keep myself steady and not be blown over.

It felt like there was an evil presence in the wind as I struggled with every step. That it was purposely trying to knock me over and ending it all then and there.

My long hair was whipping around my face. I was being pushed and battered by the wind. I yelled at the wind, "I'm not giving up!" I was crawling on my hands and knees. "Oh, praise God, praise Jesus, I found the trail," was my litany to myself as I struggled the last few hundred feet to get to my faithful car, Hazel. I noticed a man with a camera taking a picture. He must have gotten into his car and pulled out quickly, because when I arrived at the parking area, Hazel was alone.

I must have looked like a crazy person.

True to herself, Hazel started right up. Giving another prayer of gratitude, I cranked up the heater, feeling the air warm around me. My feet were tingling, slowly warming up. I had prickles of pain, like sharp needles in my hands and feet as my frozen flesh thawed.

It felt so good to be back … safe. I was charged with adrenaline from the hike and was happy and exhilarated that I had survived the night. Indeed, for me, I'd experienced a beautiful sunrise, with wispy clouds and a blue sky. It was a new day … a new beginning. I felt lucky to be alive. But now, I was looking forward to a cup of hot coffee.

Happy to leave the mountain, I headed my car south and east on Trail Ridge Road, toward Grand Lake and Denver.

At the first major intersection at the base of the road, I turned left into a 7-11 convenience store. With my twenty-dollar bill, I purchased coffee with cream, a pre-made egg salad sandwich, a bag of Funyuns, LifeSavers gummies, and an Almond Joy candy bar.

Sitting in my car eating my sandwich, I thought about my night on the mountain. I was still confused as to my purpose for my being led here. Why did the Voice in my head guide me there? I do not feel like I "accomplished" anything other than staying alive.

Starting the car, I let it warm again as I jumped out to put my trash in the dumpster.

Little did I know that the cup of coffee, egg salad sandwich, onion rings, gummies, and candy bar were to be my last meal for the next eleven days.

seven

Again, I Ask ... Why?

What kind of Game had I been pulled into?

The Game was on again. I pulled out of the parking lot back onto the road and instead of heading east toward Winter Park and home, I turned left, going north on a two-lane road. Hazel and I drove for about a half hour, the Voice urging me to continue driving. The road was no longer paved, and was now a rutted, bumpy dirt road. It did not appear to be well-traveled. I had not noticed any houses as I was driving.

I decided to turn around and made a quick right turn onto an old road. My intent was to pull in, reverse back out to the road and head back to the highway and home.

What? Suddenly, the car drove forward and went straight into a ditch. I tried to accelerate the car in reverse, but my tires slid in the mud, slipping deeper into the creek. What was once a road or bridge was now washed away and I sat wedged between the creek banks. Unable to go forward or backward, I was trapped.

I opened my car door, getting out to look at how stuck I was. It looked bad. I had at least a foot or more of embankment to drive out of, in the mud! The flowing creek water was about eight inches deep. I placed rocks in front of the wheels, hoping to create traction and tried again. The width of the creek was about three feet wider than the length of my car. There was not enough space to get traction, or the speed I would need to drive my car out.

It would take a tow truck to pull me out of this creek. I was not going home. I felt crushed after all I had been through the night before. It was a cruel twist of fate to be in this dire situation.

I was without communication.   My first reaction was panic. No one knew where I was. I did not have my cell phone to call for help. Two days earlier I had stopped at a store in downtown Cherry Creek. Playing the Game and listening to the Voice, I had left my cell phone in the store's dumpster. I had no reason as to why I was compelled to do that.

I'd not been thinking, Now, I was without communication.

I am stranded ... truly stranded.

I did not feel lost because I knew I had driven straight north on the road for about fifteen miles. I really felt like I was a puppet doing whatever the puppeteer told me and look where it had gotten me.

What kind of Game had I been pulled into?

Getting back into my car, I sat in the passenger seat and assessed the condition of my body. I saw that I was in pretty good shape. That is, if I ignored the deep cut on my right-hand ring finger that already looked infected and was green with pus. My left eye was bloodshot, and the flesh around the corner of my eye was red with an abrasion where the tree branch I walked into had poked it.

Multiple other cuts and scrapes on my legs and arms were mostly superficial. My feet still felt tender, but no lasting effects of hypothermia. The good news was that I hadn't broken anything.

Now, I needed to focus on my finger that was swollen, red, and obviously infected. Holding the injured finger in my left hand. I gave myself Reiki. I could feel tingling in my finger, a pulsing energy. After a few hours, the swelling and redness were gone, and the cut was healing.

This is good, right?

I was amazed at the power of healing and light that I was connected to. I knew this cut would have become a big problem with infection had I not done the Reiki healing.

But I was not prepared for my spiritual awakening and connection to the divine and supernatural realm that was yet to come.

I was not afraid ... not yet. I still had hope that somehow I would be rescued.

I honked the horn over and over until it stopped working.

Turning the ignition, I heard just a small click: dead battery. Barefoot, I got out of Hazel. Popping open the front hood, I checked the battery connections and gave it Reiki. I had read that another healer had successfully charged a dead car battery.

Why not me?

Holding my hands on the battery, I tried channeling energy, but I was not really feeling the flow. Maybe I was too distracted standing in the cold water. I shut the hood, climbed back into the car, and turned the ignition: just a small click.

Maybe I will try later.

Taking an inventory of what was in the car, I found a few items that were helpful. In the glove box I found a space blanket and a small transistor radio, and flashlight. In my purse was a lighter, a couple of cigarettes, and a half bag of LifeSavers gummies. The backseat held a box with family photos and old letters, and a board game, *The Worst-Case Scenario Survival Game.*

Coincidence? I do not think so. Is this the Game that keeps popping up—a survival of the worst kind?

What kind of Game had I been pulled into?

eight

Family Memories Are My Companions

Would I survive this ordeal?
Would I live to see my kids again?

I assumed it would be safe to drink the water this high in the mountains because it was flowing. Making short hikes into the trees, I gathered kindling and wood, always staying in sight of my car and where I could see the road.

Now, circle-walking became my norm. I do not know why. What the meaning of doing this? It was just plain weird. I was compelled to walk around beetle killed pine. After a few hours of circles, I returned to build my campfire.

I thought back to happy times with Paige and Ryan, and our family camping trips. I was glad for the memories and the basic knowledge to start a fire easily that I had learned as a Girl Scout leader. Silently, I gave thanks again.

Standing next to the blazing fire, I warmed my body.

At least, I'm not dealing with frostbite.

The high hope I had of being found began to dwindle.

The average low temperature here in the Arapaho National Forest in June is 37.4 degrees Fahrenheit at night and maximum of 71.6 degrees Fahrenheit during the day.

This was the second week of June, and it was freezing cold. The fire felt wonderful, and I did not feel so alone.

Staring into the fire, I reassessed my situation, wondering how this was going to turn out. Where I was stranded was not visible from the road. As the reality of my predicament set in, a dark cloud started forming in my head. My high hopes of being found began to dwindle.

I was missing my children, Thomas, and our Boxer dogs, Bob and Boomer, brothers from the same litter. Most of my hikes had been with all of them. Being alone and stranded was hard to face. Just a few weeks ago, we almost spent a night on the mountain when we got turned around on a trail without flashlights. With Bob and Boomer's help, we blindly made our way on the trail.

On that night I was scared. In fact, I was terrified as the shadows of trees and rocks looked like spooky sentinels. Visually, they were menacing and the fear of mountain lions attacking us kept popping up in my mind. But then I had Thomas and Bob and Boomer with me.

We found hiking sticks that helped us stay on the trail and avoid large rocks and boulders that night. I remembered Thomas's calm assurance that we were safe, and we would eventually make it back to our car.

That was then … this is now. I sat by the fire for hours, troubled thoughts flooding my mind as the day slowly turned to nightfall.

Why am I here?

As I sat, my thoughts turned to my family and our home. Life had been difficult lately. It felt like there was an evil presence in the home we were renting. Anger and arguments ensued. Thomas was irritable, and we clashed over parenting and the kids' chores.

A friend recommended we have the house cleansed with sage and rid it of any bad juju that was lingering within the walls. When she was in the basement, she determined there was an evil entity attached to an old wooden chest that was filled with Victorian-era clothes and memorabilia. Her recommendation was to remove it.

It seemed reasonable to me, and I sent it away with her. My mom was livid that her antique chest had been spirited away. She told me I had been conned, but I was glad to have it gone.

Paige and Ryan are everything I could hope for. Both have pure hearts: kind, beautiful souls inside and out. The moment I held each child after giving birth, I fell completely in love and bonded. Their childhood years went by so fast, many wonderful times and memories that I cherished. I was grateful they were living at home with us part-time.

I assumed the kids were fine. They had a lot of freedom because they were responsible, good kids.

Now, as young adults, they wanted to be with their friends and have more independence. I did not spend as much time with them as I would have liked. They had their own vehicles. Paige and Ryan were free to come and go to my house or to their father's place. It was a comfort to know the kids had the love and support of their grandparents on both sides.

Would my disappearance bring the family closer together?

Paige was a nanny for two small children and attended classes at the university's main downtown campus. She had always been a sweet daughter, so intelligent with a funny, sharp wit that made us laugh.

At this moment, I could feel … sense … her sadness and it was unbearable to feel so helpless, unable to be with her. I thought of her hopes and dreams and wondered if I would survive to share her life.

When Paige was just a baby, she loved to listen to music and moved with an innate rhythm. I enrolled her in tap, jazz, and **Skippy became her medicine.** ballet classes when she was three years old. For ten years, she spent hours practicing and was part of a performing dance company. It was always a delight to see her perform. The time came when she decided to stop dancing and spend her time caring for her American Paint horse, Skippy.

Skippy became her medicine after the trauma of the divorce. Skippy had been "cowboyed," subjected to harsh treatment in the past. She was skittish at times, but with Paige's love and care, she came to trust her and they bonded. For a few years she spent most of her free time at the barn, taking lessons and riding with her friends.

Paige used her own money to pay for the costs of breeding Skippy and named her newborn colt Tsunami. She was so proud of the little foal. We were both heartbroken when we had to sell her horses.

When we purchased Skippy, I did not realize it would be so costly. Boarding fees were expensive as well as lessons and veterinarian bills, but it was worth every penny. The sheer joy on her face was a memory of a lifetime. I had always held the hope that someday, somehow, she would get to live her dream of riding again.

I could see her sitting on her horse, laughing, smiling and happy. Tears slid down my cheeks as I thought back. I felt physical pain in my heart with the fear of never seeing her again. I wondered if I would ever be able to tell her again how very much I love her, or how precious she was to me.

My tears continued to come to my eyes again as I thought about Ryan. I could picture his face so clearly. He had matured so much in the last few years.

He liked his downtime and was an avid gamer. He was a night owl and gaming was his thing. We set up the basement with a room for him to escape to. In his free time, he gamed with his friends. It was comforting to know he was safe at home and we welcomed his friends' visits.

When they were with me, I enjoyed making breakfast. They especially loved Philly cheesesteak sandwiches. Being teens, they appreciated any food, gobbling down anything in their reach! They were a nice group of kids, and surprisingly diverse, considering he went to a predominantly white suburban school. I was proud of Ryan: a good friend, a team player, and a heart of gold. I loved and understood him.

I did not mind that Ryan preferred to be playing his Xbox. He had an online group he played with regularly, players from all over the country … always interested in military games, building military planes, tanks, and ships. He was creative and would spend hours putting Lego pieces together from kits. Paintball was his action sport.

I remembered a fun day when Thomas and I took him and a few friends to the outdoor paintball course. Afterward, Ryan had marble-sized welts on his body, but he loved it, and was always eager to play again. Once we brought a picnic and drinks for Ryan and his friends to enjoy during breaks.

Ryan could race a car before he could ride a bike!

When I was paying for Ryan at the entrance booth, Boomer and Bob wound around me with their leashes, tripping me, and I fell flat on my back. Everyone had a great laugh. It seemed to happen in slow motion. As I thought of it now, it still brought a smile to my face.

Ryan was the "builder," a whiz at putting things together. A car lover since he was a tot, he loved to play with his Hot Wheels and later raced quarter midgets. At five years old, he was a better driver than most adults. He sped around the racetrack at thirty mph, skillfully guiding his race car, passing the other racers. I realized that Ryan could race a car before he could ride a bike!

As I sat here, I remembered the time he was racing and my heart leaped into my throat when his five-year-old self flipped his car. I ran onto the track. When he got out of his car, he was laughing. So much for the mom worrier in me.

Ryan was now working part-time at a restaurant while going to high school and had recently restored his four-wheel-drive Jeep. Our bond was strong. I knew he was worried about me. I could sense it right now. I felt so unsettled being far away from him.

How I wished I could be back in that place in time with Ryan, and have a chance to hug him and tell him how much I love him.

In fact, I loved both my kids to an extreme, sometimes being a helicopter mom. My own childhood lacked parental love and attention, and this influenced my overzealous love and affection for them.

Would I survive this ordeal? Live to see my kids again?

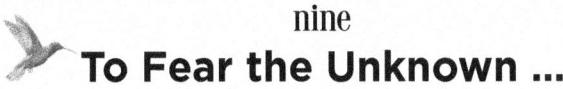

nine
To Fear the Unknown ...

*Once again, I had that "uh-oh" feeling
that something was wrong.*

Snuffing out the friendly fire, I felt alone again. The memories
of my family had been welcoming. This was the second night
without contact. No one knew where I was. Discouraged and sad,
filled with anxiety, fleeting thoughts of "what-ifs?" raced through
my mind.

What if a bear or mountain lion was watching me, waiting to
attack? What if I was never found?

I heard distant sounds of people laughing and the engines of
ATVs. They would never hear me yelling for help. I imagined the
fun they were having and felt even more isolated. Trying to rein
in my uneasiness of feeling watched, I decided **My stomach was**
the least of my worries were animal attacks. In **growling loudly.**
all my years of hiking, the only animals I had seen were moose,
deer, elk, wild turkey, and other small critters.

I was hungry. My stomach was growling loudly. At least I had
plenty of water, which would take the edge off my hunger.
Tomorrow I would look for something edible. For now, I went
back to the safety of my car.

It was a long night of endless worry. I tossed and turned all night, hoping my restlessness would at least create warmth with the movements, but I was still so cold. The space blanket failed to keep the cold out.

The back of Hazel had seats that could fold down, making a space large enough for sleeping. The thin gray carpet was old, dirty, and covered in dog hair. It was uncomfortable and I missed my bed. At fifteen years old, with over 100,000 miles, Hazel showed no signs that she was ready for retirement.

Other than an ongoing transmission problem that we finally fixed, Hazel had proven to be a decent used car. Turning on the transistor radio, I tuned into a country station and listened for a little while. I did not want to drain the batteries. It seemed like batteries were always going dead around me: flashlights and the car battery. I had to get a jump-start on my car battery several times recently. Thomas had not had time to replace the battery. The car's horn would have been a great tool to alert someone/ anyone of my location.

I prayed and asked for help to get back home. Once again, I had that "uh-oh" sensation that something was wrong. I felt I was being watched, vulnerable sitting prey to who knows what. I convinced myself it must be an animal, maybe a deer. Making sure my doors were locked, I stared out in the dark night searching but finding nothing.

I was cold and scared but finally fell asleep.

What will tomorrow bring?

ten
Homesick

All I could do was wait.

June 11, 2010 | **DAY THREE – The Blizzard**

I woke up to my car windows covered in ice. Scraping a peep-hole to look out, I saw that it was snowing, apparently blizzard conditions, with the wind blowing large snowflakes sideways.

Climbing from the back of Hazel to the front seat, my body began to shiver from the cold. I had to urinate urgently, but I did not want to get out of the car in the storm and step into the creek. I found a bottle and peed in it. It was awkward but I managed. How simple this was for a man!

The snow would keep me in the car, a prisoner of the storm, unable to build another fire. All the wood I had gathered was now wet and buried in snow.

I ate the last of my LifeSavers gummies, chewing each piece slowly, savoring the tangy sweetness. My stomach was growling for more food, and I was thirsty. I realized that I had not taken my daily medications for five days now. A decision I made on my own after I started taking a combination of DHEA and a hormone com-pound was to stop taking everything else. I was feeling as if I had more energy.

My medications were the least of my worries, although I did wonder if I would have side effects.

Now, I just wanted food, a cup of coffee, and to be home safe with my family. I needed to be doing something that would help me get out of this mess, but there was nothing proactive I could do.

The snow fell all day and night and the water in the creek was slowly rising. I stayed in the car, turning on the transistor radio, listening to the announcer's voice talk

All I could do was wait.

about the storm, happenings around town, and then playing country songs. I really loved music and country music always was a favorite. I like the heartfelt stories told in the songs.

My mind was in constant worry, rolling thoughts over and over about my family and how I had really let them down by just running off. I was caught up with the Voice and the Game and was painfully aware I had made serious mistakes.

I did not have much hope that I would be found in the creek, out of sight from the road. I decided my best course of action was to walk back out on the road that I drove in on. Having a plan gave me a little hope. It was something I could focus my mind on while I was stranded in the blizzard-embraced car. As the storm raged on, all I could do was wait.

I spent part of the day reading the cards in *The Worst-Case Scenario Survival Game,* a game of my niece's that landed in my car while helping my mom with her recent move. Most of the scenarios were not relevant to my situation but I did learn a few tips that would help me later. Interesting that I had it in my car.

The setup was similar to *Trivial Pursuit*, where you picked a card and on the card's reverse side it had several answers to choose from if you were in a dire situation. I got bored reading the game cards so I reached for the hatbox. Letters, cards, and pictures of my relatives were inside. I had found the hatbox in the wooden chest that my Aunt Bernadette brought over one day.

I pulled out letters written in Spanish to my great-aunt Lucy from her husband Al when he was serving in the Korean War. I could make out a few words here and there, always ending with "Vaya con Dios" … *Go with God*. When Al was in the war, he suffered a brain injury. I did not know the details of his injury, how severe the damage was, but the letters surprised me. Although Al was friendly and always gave a hug when you saw him, he seldom spoke. He used to communicate quite well before the injury. There were some two dozen letters and cards.

There were other items obviously dear to her: her son's childhood Bible, a large, framed photo of Al wearing his military uniform, crocheted lace doilies, and a pretty, little ceramic dolphin painted blue that I really liked.

I do not think it was a coincidence that I had pulled the hatbox out and left it in the car for me to find now. I sensed that I was meant to be here … just me and the pictures … and the memories.

The pictures were of my grandparents, aunts, uncles, cousins, mom, brother, sister, and myself. One was of me in the third grade. I was wearing a white sailor shirt with a blue tie, and my hair was cut uneven and sticking up as if it had not been brushed. I looked like I just got out of bed. Other than looking disheveled, I appeared to be healthy and happy with an endearing crooked smile on my face. The photo did not reveal the trauma in my life.

The neglect was not intentional, rather just the fallout of our family's situation: A single mom who worked two and three jobs to support us and was never home in the morning to see that we were dressed properly, had eaten a decent breakfast, and got off to school okay.

I sighed and turned the picture over. In my childish writing, I had written, "I Love You" to great-aunt Lucy. She was so kind to me. I loved to visit her; she always called me "my little doll." I thought it was funny because I did not play with dolls. She always looked so pleased to see me and I enjoyed the attention she gave me. I felt special, as she singled me out from all the other children, and I enjoyed the little trinkets she gave me to play with.

They were now my companions.

Aunt Lucy was a very small lady, only about four feet tall. One of her shoes had a built-up wedge on the shoe sole at least six inches high. Today she would be called a 'little person.' When she was a small child, she fell off a countertop, breaking her hip, causing her to be handicapped her whole life. She had one son that died at 18 years old in a Jeep accident.

She had a life of tragedy, but Aunt Lucy was always laughing and smiling. Her face was made up with thick white powder, bright rouge spots on her cheeks, and red lipstick. She reminded me of a painted china doll. I felt honored to have her mementos and now I especially enjoyed looking at the pictures. They were now my companions.

I gathered all the letters and pictures, putting them back in the hatbox. Reclining back in the seat, I shut my eyes, holding my bare foot in both hands, and feeling the energy begin to flow once again.

eleven
Memories of Mom

My hatbox memories continued.
Thoughts of my mom filled my head.

Shortly after my Reiki attunement, my mother, Sally, moved into our house. She was a workaholic and now suffered from Type 2 Diabetes and hypertension. Her life was consumed with running her bookkeeping business and managing my brother's various businesses … working long hours.

Before she moved in with us, I used to stop by her office and do errands for her a few times a week. With her poor health and the aging factor, I was now doing her grocery shopping, cooking some of her meals, taking her to doctor's appointments, picking up her dry cleaning or any other errands necessary.

Both Thomas and I enjoyed my mom. Unfortunately, we lived on opposite ends of town so when I visited her, it was a forty- to sixty-minute trip one way, depending on traffic.

Mom was a mom other kids loved, even carrying the "favorite aunt" title. She would do anything for her children and the children of our large family. We were her world. All the childhood trauma and suffering growing up did not dim the love and respect my siblings and I held for her.

She was a strong, independent woman—brilliant and generous to a fault—but a sucker for the wrong type of men. She overcame many challenges in her life and worked hard to achieve the earnings she made as a business owner.

During one of my visits, I noticed she was not feeling well. I had her lie down on her bed and took her blood sugar reading. Pricking her finger, I squeezed the drop of blood onto the test strip and stuck it into the glucose monitor. Her reading was 48; she appeared incoherent. I knew a 48 reading was dangerously low blood sugar level.

Immediately I called 911 and told them her blood sugar reading. "See if she can drink some orange or apple juice. Stay with her until the ambulance arrives. It has already been called."

She was now unconscious. I placed my hands on her heart, calling to her to wake up. She opened her eyes and looked straight at me … yet she looked as if she did not know it was me with her. I was shocked. Her eyes were black as coal and I did not understand what was going on with her.

Was she dying?

I thought it would take about fifteen minutes for the ambulance to arrive. Placing my hands on her upper chest and then moving them down to her upper stomach, I began channeling Reiki energy to her body.

After several minutes, her shirt was soaked, and my hands were wet with the release of moisture. Then I heard the paramedics coming through the front door and down the hallway into Mom's bedroom. At once, I stepped aside and handed off the glucose monitor with the 48 reading. One paramedic gave her another test and the other performed vitals on her.

Her blood sugar was now 98!

I know that the Reiki had helped her. She was coming out of her delirium and was fully conscious. Taking sips of apple juice, she looked around in surprise at the firefighters.

"Why are you here?" she asked.

"Your daughter called us because of the extreme drop in your blood sugar. With her help, you seem better. We recommend you see your primary doctor soon."

Mom was admitted to the hospital a few days later. The diagnosis: kidney failure. She was stabilized in the hospital but given the bad news that she would need to go to dialysis three days a week. Someone would have to take her for treatment and bring her home. Her diet would be restricted, and she should not be working. She could not live alone anymore.

That someone would be me. Thomas and I told her she was welcome to live with us. Paige and Ryan were excited that she would be with us.

It did not sit well with her at all. She was not sure. She felt like all independence had been whisked away.

With the combination of my chronic fatigue, lupus, and fibro-myalgia, I had been out of the workplace for over a year. I helped my sister with child care for her young daughter, Kristiana. Mom would be welcome in my home as well.

When she was released from the hospital, we moved her into our house. We had a spare room we used as an office and turned it into her bedroom. At first, she was a cranky patient at times. I understood. It isn't easy to stay positive and happy when you don't feel well. I had a lot of compassion for her and knew she missed working and staying busy.

At that time, my own health was responding to the Reiki treatments. I was feeling better mentally and physically. Mom had responded to the few minutes of Reiki that I gave her when she was unconscious.

Why not keep doing it?

I began giving her Reiki treatments three or four times a week. With that and the homemade meals, her crankiness subsided. Her humor began to resurface as we drove to and from her dialysis appointments.

After a few months Mom was starting to feel better. The pain in her legs from childhood polio subsided, but she hated going for her dialysis. I would sit with her throughout each session, filling out the paperwork to check her in and see that she was being taken care of. She would settle into a large lounge chair with her own TV to watch while her blood was pumped and cleansed through the machine.

She hated being there; so did I. The smell of the facility was unpleasant, and with my self-Reiki treatments, my sense of smell had become more acute. The facility smelled of blood and urine and chemicals. Many times, feeling nauseated, I left the room and walked outside for fresh air.

Each treatment left her pale and weak. She tried to be brave and not complain, as she leaned on me for help. When polio overtook her at seven, she vowed to be as independent as she could be, not wanting sympathy or pity from others.

Thinking about her made me appreciate her will to survive and succeed. I imagined that she must be so worried. I had never just disappeared without a word to anyone, and I kept in contact with her at least weekly, sometimes daily. I had the utmost respect for her. She was a survivor.

She married at 18. By the time she was 21, she was the mother of two and entered the divorced working world and was the sole support for my brother and sister.

Mom worked two jobs to support us, paying her parents to babysit us until my sister Jayne took over at nine years old. I had been the afterthought mistake from one of her ex's visitation times. I was three years old when Mom married again … a man with three kids.

With her at work, we became children raising children. Jayne was responsible for babysitting five small children and was like a little mother to all of us.

If Mom were here, she would tell me that I could get through this … that I was strong. I imagined she was probably talking on the phone to Jayne or one of her sisters. In our family, a favorite pastime was to talk for hours on the phone, gossiping. There was always drama going on and just idle talk.

Most likely the phones were lit up with speculation about my disappearance.

I got along well with my relatives and liked them. A memory was seared in my preadolescent self when I overheard a relative say to my mother, "Oh, Sally, Kelly is so homely! The poor thing! Can't you do something to help her?"

That remark made me feel self-conscious and overly critical of myself and my appearance.

I have always been able to see something positive in people, regardless of superficial beauty or lack thereof. Really, who can control how one looks? I have met attractive people where their beauty was only skin-deep, and their character left much to be desired.

Those words taught me not to judge people just by their looks. I made up for my perceived ugliness by being nice, friendly, and funny. This ugly duckling eventually grew out of her awkwardness and unkemptness.

The fourth month that mom was living with us, I drove her to an appointment with her kidney specialist. While in the waiting room to check in, I had a very strange encounter that left me utterly drained. A very old, bent-over man with a piercing stare and heavily wrinkled face came just inches from me and my three-year-old niece. What I heard him say was, "You two look very nice."

The energy around him was weird. The hair on my arms rose. I immediately moved away, pulling my niece with me. Smirking, he looked directly at us and stood straight up. His appearance transformed into a younger man! I could not believe my eyes!

Frightened, I moved myself and Kristiana as far away from him as possible and we sat down by Mom waiting to be called into an exam room. I felt sick, my energy completely zapped, sucked out of my body. Kristiana slumped like a rag doll in the chair. This man was an energy vampire.

Mom was called into the exam room, and we were up and followed her in. The nurse took her vitals and bloodwork and left.

Her doctor walked into the exam room studying her chart. Looking up at her, he asked, "How do you feel?"

"I am feeling better, but I hate the dialysis treatments," was her blunt response. Now, the doctor studied her. Peering over his glasses, he said, "Well, I am surprised to say this, but your kidney function is good enough to take you off dialysis. Whatever you have been doing is working and I'm pleased to say it's remarkable!"

Mom was happy at the news, but with a huge smile, she questioned his statement. "Really? I can stop the treatments?!"

The doctor said he had never seen a case where this had happened and asked, "What have you been doing?"

Mom replied, "My daughter takes care of me. Kelly has had me on a restricted diet, and she does Reiki on me."

He turned to me and asked, "What is Reiki? I've not heard of it."

"It's basically hands-on healing," was my response. "I channel healing energy with my hands and pray over the part of the body I'm working on. There is a little more to it, but that's the gist of it."

Now, he spoke to Mom. "I'm happy for you … that you're better. I'll need you to come back in a few weeks to recheck your kidney function."

A few months later, Mom moved out of our home. She said she was needed to help run Roger's businesses, and she felt great.

What could I say? She was a fiercely independent woman who wanted to live her life as she wanted. With her new clean bill of health, she could get back to work that gave her life purpose.

She was happy. For me, I was reluctant to encourage her to go, believing she needed more time to heal.

Her time with us was a gift … for me … for Thomas … for our kids.

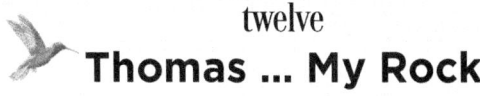

twelve
Thomas ... My Rock

Keeping up with anyone was not his style.

Encompassed by the blizzard, I was filled with nostalgia and homesick for my family … for Thomas. I thought of the ten years we had been together. I loved him and was fortunate to have him in my life. He had been so supportive from the time we first met. He was my rock. My fervent prayer was that Thomas would be there for Paige and Ryan, and help them get through this difficult time.

The power of Reiki entered my mind again. I remembered how Reiki had helped Thomas. One time, I felt compelled to work on Thomas' throat. His lymph nodes were enlarged, as big as golf balls, although he was not ill with any throat issues.

He reclined on the couch with his eyes closed. I held my hand over his throat chakra and spun it counterclockwise, then clockwise. Placing my hands on his throat, I felt energy coursing through them, starting with the tingle in my palms and what felt like a constant flow of electricity coming out of each palm into his throat. Thomas was lying down on his back while I sat at his side, channeling energy to what felt like a solid blockage in his throat. He said, "I can feel the bile running back down my throat. It's nasty." I was not surprised. And yes, bile was nasty stuff.

He also revealed that he saw flashes of purple as his lymph nodes drained.

For the next few days, Thomas cleansed and processed this blockage. He told me he was feeling strong emotions of anger and later told me he felt wretched and hopeless. The energy moved through him, his healing crisis ended, and his lymph nodes returned to normal size, and his moodiness went away. When I offered to work on other parts of his body, he took a pass. The strong emotions that followed had been a surprise.

It was a powerful healing, moving a lot of old, stuck energy. Thomas was amazed with the results. His throat felt better, and the chipmunk-looking appearance on his neck disappeared.

Thomas was supportive of my newfound passion, although he seldom accepted when I offered a treatment. I know how he truly loved Paige and Ryan and thought of them as his own. It was a big change to take on the role of parent and stepfather.

He helped with the kids and shared his love of nature and hiking. His confidence and keen belief of life in general and especially how he made me laugh was one of my favorite things. His kindness as an advocate for animals, the environment, and non-attachment to material, superficial trappings was a huge plus.

This was a big change for me and the kids. Coming from the suburbs where the median income was $125,000 a year, consumption was in overdrive and *keeping up with the Joneses* was the suburban lifestyle.

With Thomas, keeping up with anyone was not his style.

We got along well and were alike in many ways, complementing each other's strengths. I was happy he loved Paige and Ryan and bonded with them. It had not been an easy transition to be a stepfather and virtually start over in midlife.

He had been successful in business before we met and took a two-year timeout from the everyday work grind. Looking for balance in his life, the sea called to him. *Aquanimity* became his new home—a 41-foot Class C Hunter sailboat. The intercoastal waterways and Atlanctic Ocean became a passageway to greater waters.

The stock market crash in 2000-2001 delivered a redirect. Time to go back to work.

We went through some hard times, both of us trying to recover financially, starting over together.

How could I have just taken off for the mountains in Hazel without telling him? He had asked me the week before why I was off. I could not tell him. I did not understand it myself.

thirteen
Native Roots

Have I been pulled to the dark side?

It was another cold, restless night. Imagining myself no longer in the lives of my family filled me with sorrow. I felt helpless. There was no way anyone would find me in this storm. At least I had Hazel's shelter, although no heater.

I desperately missed Paige and Ryan. My worry was in overdrive. All I have ever wanted was to provide a happy, safe, and loving home for them. I thought about Paige. What a sensitive and loving soul she was, so trusting in others. Ryan, always the peacemaker, was generous and easygoing. Both were just starting their lives as young adults. They needed me. I could not help but feel like I had failed.

About a year ago, I felt called to go to a metaphysical fair. I asked Paige if she would like to go. "Great," she said. "Yes, it sounds interesting." We drove the hour-long trip from Denver to Colorado Springs on a Sunday, the last day of the fair. I thought it would be fun to spend the day with Paige, maybe sit in and listen to various speakers.

One speaker's topic was "Channeling Your Angel Helpers." Later that night, I channeled my great-grandmother Carolina and wrote a short note asking for help. How I did it in Spanish, I'm not sure. I don't speak, read, or write it, but I did then. I fell asleep and when I awoke, I had drawn an image of a fountain. I was surprised at the detail of the picture and wondered what it meant.

And when did I draw it if I was asleep?

I could see that Paige was taking it all in, not missing a thing. We enjoyed browsing around the event center, visiting different booths with items to sell like crystals, books, clothing, artwork, and jewelry.

Sitting at a row of tables on a stage above the floor of the vendors was a woman dressed in turquoise. Her presence was regal and inviting. Curious to know what service she offered, we walked up to her table. Immediately she said, "Oh, so you're a turtle person." Obviously, she had noticed my necklace with my little turquoise and silver turtle pendant. As she was identifying me as a turtle person, I looked up and saw she also wore a beautiful turtle necklace, much larger than my own with a very nice turquoise stone. Laughing, I said, "Yes, turtles are one of my favorites."

When I feel nervous, I tend to laugh. I was a little uncomfortable at being studied. I asked about her bulletin offering shamanic classes. "What is shamanic?" I had never heard the word before. Something about her was compelling. I thought maybe it was because she was Native American. I always admired the Native American culture and concept of all things being connected.

She looked like an Indian queen. She appeared to be in her 80s. Her hair was in long braids on each side of her head. She reminded me in a fleeting way of my own grandmother who had passed from this world sixteen years ago. We introduced ourselves. "I'm Kelly and this is my daughter, Paige. This is the first fair we've attended, so everything is new to us," I said.

Introducing herself as Meredith, she asked, "Are you Native American?" Flattered, I replied, "Yes, my grandfather was part Apache Indian." I did not go into details, but the story was Grandpa's great-great-grandmother was abducted by the Apache and bore children. My beloved grandfather had passed ten years ago but I could clearly see his chiseled features, put a headdress on him, add a horse, and there would be no doubt. He was Native American.

It sounded pagan.

Meredith said, "Yes, I thought that you must have some Native American blood in you. My classes will be starting in just a few weeks. You might really enjoy learning about Native American ways. I will be having a Full Moon Fire Ceremony next week at my house in Denver. Both you and your daughter are welcome to come and learn more." She added, "It's almost time to shut down for the night. If you want to do a reading, we can do it then."

I grabbed a flyer and said, "Yes, I'll be calling to get more details." I had never been to a Full Moon Fire Ceremony, nor did I have a clue to what happened at one. It sounded pagan. In my limited knowledge, the image of people dancing came to mind. Was it safe? It seemed so different from the conservative church services I had always attended. Meredith seemed normal, nice, and trustworthy. She revealed she had been a shaman for more than thirty years. Paige and I decided it would not hurt to go and have a new experience, even if I was apprehensive.

At the fair were a variety of services: Reiki healers, tarot card readers, astrologists, palm readers, psychics, rolfing, quantum energetics. It was all new to me, but timing was everything. And I was open-minded and thought it would be harmless to get a reading … explore a little.

We talked on the way home about the fair and class we attended. It had been a good day. I enjoyed spending the afternoon together.

Lately, we had drifted apart. She was busy with her life: going to college; working as a nanny, caring for a baby and toddler; spending time with her boyfriend from high school and other friends. I gave her space and freedom to basically do as she wished, as she was now an adult.

Paige was incredibly smart. I know every mother thinks this about her child, but in school she tested at 135 IQ. In ninth grade, she had been nominated to participate in the school's prestigious I.B. program. After serious consideration, she declined when we discussed the advanced placement classes she would be taking, the extra homework, and the stress of our parenting schedule of a split home.

I understood and supported her choice to have a more stress-free high school experience and join activities that would be fun. The school's equestrian program and cheerleading/dance squad won her attention. We enjoyed going to her high school games when she cheered.

After our outing to the fair, I wondered if I was setting a good example going there. After all, I was a Christian. And now I was taking her to the Full Moon Fire Ceremony. I felt guilty that I had somehow betrayed the religion I grew up with and fostered in my children. Paige and Ryan had attended a private Christian school for five years and had only been exposed to protestant teaching and Christian churches.

Paige had liked Meredith and wanted to get a tarot card reading when I went for mine. I called Meredith a few days later and booked an appointment for a reading for both of us.

The following week we arrived at Meredith's home. She lived in a nice neighborhood with large custom homes and acre lots, a private lake, and walking trail across from her house. Having read her bio, I felt more comfortable. She had a doctorate and an extensive teaching background.

We stood at her doorstep and rang her doorbell. A young man answered the door and came outside. He seemed shifty to me, nervous, guilty of something. He said Meredith would be right out. I later learned that he was boarding at her house and things had not been going well. Meredith did not approve of his lifestyle and wanted him to move out.

When she came to the door and welcomed us inside, she had us stand in the entryway as she smudged us with burning sage. The three of us sat in her dining room and talked a little. She asked if we would like a cup of hot tea, which we accepted. We decided Paige would have her reading first and she invited me to sit and wait my turn in her sunroom.

Upon entering the room, I was surrounded by many beautiful plants and turtles placed throughout the room. Native American artwork hung on the walls. There was beautiful Indian pottery that looked handmade. It was an inviting place with a flowing waterfall in the corner.

Sitting on a loveseat, I gazed out at her backyard. I noticed one of her trees had a large white mask nailed to it with black eye holes and a red mouth, about four feet tall and three and one-half feet wide. I thought it kind of strange that it was outside. I guessed this was where she had the Full Moon Fire Ceremony.

Her question caught me off guard.

Paige walked into the sunroom with Meredith. It was time for my reading. A few things I remembered from the reading were that my cards indicated a connection or importance to Judaism, Native American, and goddess energy.

She looked at my palms and asked, "What is your interest, men or women?" Surprised by her question, I replied, "I'm heterosexual." She replied, "Yes, that is what your palm says as well. I was just confirming." I assumed this was something that she asked everybody to give her insight if there were issues around gender and self-identity. Her question caught me off guard. I thought it was odd to ask.

We chatted about ourselves. I told her a little bit about my family, Thomas, Paige, and Ryan, and that I had been sick with health problems, recently becoming a Reiki healer. She was very sweet and perceptive, reminding me again of my grandmother. I was surprised, as she appeared at least fifteen years younger than her true age.

Then she said something that seemed cryptic. She said, "I have been waiting a long time for this moment and began to doubt it would ever happen."

Immediately the subject was changed. My reading was over and we stood up to get Paige.

I explained to Meredith that money was an issue for me and as much as I would like to have more readings, I just could not afford it. She offered the shaman course at a steeply discounted rate and said, "If you're interested in making some side money, I could use some help with bookkeeping."

I was thrilled at the opportunity and said, "I could give you some Reiki treatments in exchange for your helping me out." The cost of the shaman course was $800 and then possibly a vision quest with that price to be determined later. After a quick hug and thank-you, we left Meredith's house. I asked Paige if she had a good reading. She said, "Yes, we talked about school and what I want to do for a living."

Paige and I returned to Meredith's house for the Full Moon Fire Ceremony a few weeks later. After getting smudged upon entering her house, we went into the kitchen where a few people were gathered drinking hot tea. After brief introductions, we moved into her formal living room and sat listening to Meredith explain the peace pipe ceremony.

She gave instructions to have ready a short prayer or wish to share when holding the pipe filled with loose tobacco leaf. When it was my turn, I asked for blessings for my family and world peace.

Everyone in the prayer circle included a wish of peace for all. We all moved to her backyard where she had a large fire burning. Giving everyone a small note with words to a Native American healing chant, we gathered around the fire, chanting together, and then it was over.

The Full Moon Fire Ceremony was a cool experience. There was nothing weird or scary about it. No one danced wildly. It was a very thoughtful and spiritual sharing and coming together. The song we chanted was melodic and mesmerizing, and it struck a chord of familiarity in me. I enjoyed the sound of the resonant drum being played by another guest. It felt primal and grounding. Everyone had made a prayer stick to throw into the fire at the end of our chanting. Paige and I found sticks and painted them in bright colors, adding glitter and writing out wishes on the stick. It was a nice evening and all the guests had been friendly and welcoming.

The shaman eight-week course started and there were just six of us, including Meredith, who sat with each of us as we pulled our animal spirit totem card from her deck of medicine cards. I pulled a hummingbird, and its meaning is *joy*. It conjures up magical qualities of love and opens the heart, bringing joy to those around them.

This made me happy as I have always loved hummingbirds. They always bring a smile to my face when I've seen them. Energetically they don't like discord and will quickly fly away, very similar to how I feel. With my childhood awash in violence, yelling, and fighting, it was very distressing, and I hated confrontation and contention.

We made a personal medicine bag, learned how to create a healing circle, and talked about a vision quest, where the initiate will go to a secluded spot alone, perhaps on a mountain, then fast and meditate for guidance. The vision quest can last two to four days. It can empower, humble, enlighten, and strengthen you all at once! It can do so by connecting us with the spirit and creative force within all of us, helping us figure out what we really want out of life in the process.

Sometimes your spirit animal or totem will make itself known to you. This was something we could each try at the end of the Shamanic course. Meredith had a retreat center in southern Colorado. She was involved with the Native American community and spoke highly of her many friends that she had made going to the powwows.

I helped her with organizing her records to file taxes. On one occasion, as I was sitting in her office area, nicely located by glass windows and looking out at the back of the house, I saw her grab a broom and run outside. She was waving it around, saying, "Get out, get away from here. Leave this place now!"

I did not see anybody. I looked and nothing was there. When she came back inside, she looked fierce, not someone you would want to cross. For a split second, her eyes had appeared reptilian, snake-like, but quickly returned to normal. *I must have imagined it!* I asked her what she was yelling at and chasing with the broom. She just muttered, "They knew better than to come around here, harassing."

I really came to like Meredith and enjoyed spending time with her. She was wise and fun to be around. We did yoga together, went out to lunch and I attended a few more Full Moon Fire Ceremonies and shamanic classes. She was very perceptive, inquisitive, highly educated. I was impressed and a bit envious of her large personal library.

We went down to her massage room for a Reiki treatment, passing by watercolors and drawings she had made. She showed me two drawings and asked me which one was me. One drawing was a nude woman of average build and the other was a nude woman who was chubby. I chose the picture of the woman that was average. Thinking it was a weird question, I did not give it a second thought as we entered the dimly lit room where she had a massage table set up.

It was very eerie. It sounded like an animal trying to get in.

While I was giving her a Reiki treatment, something was scratching at the window. It was very eerie. It sounded like an animal trying to get in. It did not scratch just once or twice; it was insistent. I tried to put the noise out of my mind as I channeled universal love and light. Not one to mince words, she said afterward that it gave her a cold. I thought it was the after-effect of energy that needed to be cleared.

Had I been pulled to the dark side?

fourteen

A Strange Encounter

What had I gotten myself into?

At Meredith's, I met an individual named Gabriel. He was interesting to talk to and I noticed he would always ask to "shed ego and vanity" and for world peace, when he held the peace pipe.

I thought his wish to shed vanity was a good thing. I had issues with body image. My appearance was not anything special. I was average-looking. I had browsed enough magazines and been bombarded with images of perfect women in movies and on TV. I would have liked to be beautiful.

When I first met Gabriel, he asked, "What brought you to this ceremony?" I replied, "Just curious and an interest in Native American culture. And I happened to meet Meredith at a fair."

He was polite and interested and shared a little about his own journey that brought him there. He was a seeker, on a spiritual quest to learn about Native American Shamanism and had studied Hebrew and Judaism. Gabriel knew a lot more about spirituality than I did … or at least I thought so.

He had brought two pieces of metal—one silver, one gold—and explained that one was giving and one was receiving. Passing them around the group, we each held the two metal pieces that looked like miniature dumbbells. Holding the metals, I could feel the energy moving through them.

He asked about the charm bracelet I had on my right wrist. It was given to me by Thomas with all the characters in Mandarin: a blessing bracelet. Thomas thought it was a fit for the path I seemed to be on. I barely heard Gabriel say, "I'm surprised at how old you are."

I was cautious of any friendship with men. It was said half-aloud and then as if speaking to himself, he said, "Usually he goes for someone a lot younger. This story has been played out many times."

"Who are you talking about," I asked.

Abruptly, he redirected the discussion. I never received an answer.

Later, I spoke with him on the phone about receiving a Reiki treatment and he talked about astral travel and spirituality in general. It sounded like he was in a wind tunnel, so I only heard parts of what he was saying. He asked if I drank coffee and mentioned maybe meeting for a cup of coffee at Starbucks or a glass of wine. He said coffee was okay, but for every cup of coffee you drink, you must drink twice that amount in water to stay hydrated. I never knew that, but I wasn't much of a coffee drinker anyway.

I was cautious of any friendship with men. I had been too trusting in the past. But it was clear that his interest was strictly platonic, and I felt safe. I had told Thomas about Gabriel and he seemed okay with our friendship.

Gabriel came to my house, and I gave him a Reiki treatment, one of my first paying customers. I was excited for the opportunity to grow my business and wanted to share this gift of healing with everyone. I offered him an assortment of aromatherapy essential oils to rub on his temples while he was being worked on. He chose frankincense.

I noticed that a few tears had rolled down his cheeks during treatment on the massage table. I did not mention it afterward, thinking if he wanted to share his experience he would. I would not pry. It was not a surprise to me. I remember my first Reiki session with Lisa. I cried silently, feeling a release of emotion and peacefulness, like everything was going to be okay. I felt love.

After the session, Gabriel asked me about my intention with Reiki. I replied, "To help my family and other people as much as I am able." He was an IT guy. Thomas and I thought he did websites for individuals and small companies. He said he could help me increase my Reiki business. I thought that meant he could help me build a website and market my Reiki service. He asked, "Are you sure you are ready for this?"

Excitedly, I responded, "Oh yes, I could manage a larger clientele." I thought this could be a viable business I could grow.

We had stepped outside to smoke a cigarette and walked around my yard. The house that we were renting had a lovely backyard with a peach tree, grapes, herbs, and pretty flowers. I learned that the previous owner had won an award for "best backyard landscape." The owner had created a tranquil space where I enjoyed meditating often.

Gabriel pointed to a sage shrub, saying, "Good, this will be useful." Then he stopped to admire a lilac bush and peonies, mumbling something about *when the lilacs bloom* under his breath.

As Gabriel was leaving my house walking through the kitchen and out the back door, the kitchen cupboards flew open, and all the dishes came crashing out onto the floor.

What! I was really alarmed and confused. The Reiki treatment seemed to go well, and our conversation afterward was cryptic, but this was spooky. It was something I had only seen in horror

I was not ready for anything.

movies. Picking up broken plates and glass and putting it in the trash, I wondered about Gabriel. He was mysterious but seemed like a nice person. After all, he always asked for "world peace" and to "shed ego and vanity." He had to be decent, right?

I put the unbroken dishes back in the cabinet and went to the backyard, nervously pacing and smoking a cigarette. I lit the paper with the chant I had been given at the Full Moon Fire Ceremony. It went up in flame as I held it. Dropping it on the cement, it finished burning until nothing was left but the ash of the paper I had lit. I got scared ... really scared. I could not believe what I was seeing. I rubbed my eyes. Again, I stared at the ash. Yes ... it was clearly visible.

Staring back at me was the number 666.

It was just weird how the dishes flew out of the cupboard when Gabriel left, and his cryptic question, "Are you sure you're ready for this?" I pondered what he meant ... what does *ready for this* mean?

What had I gotten myself into? The Lord's Prayer began to cycle through my mind. I needed all the protection I could get.

No, I was not ready for anything. I didn't want to be involved if it meant danger to myself or my loved ones.

I called Meredith and told her I could not attend the rest of the Shaman classes. I really hated backing out of my commitment and especially our friendship. The experience with Gabriel really rattled me.

I did not tell her about the big black truck that followed me for miles. When I felt someone was following, I started defensive driving. Turning often, expanding the route to where I was going right up to her house a few nights earlier. As soon as I reversed my direction, the truck was no longer there.

It was best to cut off any future meetings. I did not want to run into Gabriel again or be involved with any more supernatural happenings.

fifteen

Trapped by the Storm

I only knew that I was in danger.

I stayed in the car all day and night the second day. I could not see out the windows; they were covered in ice and snow. It felt like a cocoon surrounded me in silent frigid cold.

Leaning my head against the headrest, I thought about my experiences in the last nine months.

A few days after the experience with Gabriel, I completed the Reiki Master Training and Attunement. This level incorporated the spiritual plane, and I can only say I was not ready for how that would change me and my life. Reiki One and Two had not been an easy process to clear the stuck energy and relive bad memories of my past, but the rewards were worth it. I did feel better physically and emotionally. I felt lighter, as if the heavy baggage of my life journey—the sadness and trauma—was lifted and I was hopeful again. The sparkle had returned to my eyes.

After the attunement, I suddenly had clarity as to my life's purpose. I was being called to come back to spiritual faith. When I practiced Reiki, I prayed to God, Jesus, and Mary, asking for help from the angels and to be filled with divine healing light. It resonated with me to tap into the love and promise of Jesus. Even my appearance changed. I looked softer, and I was happier than I had been in a very long time.

Immediately following the master attunement, I perceived my world in a different way. Suddenly I noticed numbers and patterns of numbers. There was a connection to a higher wisdom that had me doing some strange things. It hit me like a wave crashing over me.

I was hearing the Voice telling me to go to certain places, take road trips using maps, sort of a Game—and not telling anyone what I was doing. I did not know how to play or what the rules were or why I was called to do the strange things I began doing. I only knew that I was in danger, and something was after me.

About a week later, an uncle died and I planned to attend the funeral in Trinidad, Colorado. I decided it would be best if I had the freedom to take my time and drive alone to the funeral, almost two hundred miles away. Roundtrip driving time would be close to six hours. The morning of the funeral, I dressed in business casual attire: black dress slacks; blue sleeveless top; and leather Keds.

When I stopped for gas, as I was standing in line at the cash register, the Voice told me to buy a map of Denver and the surrounding area. I had intended to hop on I-25 and drive south; a map wasn't necessary. I had driven the route many times. Trying to understand why I would do this, the Voice told me that I was being followed and I needed to take backroads all the way there. Or, at least, that was my interpretation. Someone was after me … again.

In a panic, I called a psychic I had met at the metaphysical fair. I told her I was scared and thought something evil was after me. She told me to write down and then say the *White Light Protection Prayer*:

*The light of God surrounds me, the Love of God
enfolds me. Wherever I am, God is.*

"And for protection, Kelly, I want you to imagine yourself in a
clear bubble of light and pray the *Divine Order:*"

*I surround myself with Christ's light. I ask for
the highest, the truth, only the best for all those
concerned.*

I felt more clear-headed and safer after praying these words. The
psychic's parting words were, "Remember you are a child of God,
and nothing can harm you; the power of love trumps all evil."

I drove I-85 getting on and off I-25 onto Colorado 105 then
Old Denver Road back to I-25 and south to Garden of the Gods
Road. Passing through the park, I pulled over and admired the
amazing rock formations. The gardens felt like a sacred, holy place.
I stopped in the visitor center, used the restroom, and browsed
around the pictures of the rocks and learned the different names
of the rock formations.

According to the exhibits at the Garden of the Gods Visitor and
Nature Center, the rock formations were created millions of years
ago. The formation, and much of the Rockies, is on a fault line
that caused the slabs of rock to be tilted vertically into "fins" as
the tectonic plates moved. The rocks get their red color from the
hematite in the rock.

Even knowing how they were made, seeing them for the first time
was just so unbelievable. It felt as if they were dropped from outer
space.

I pulled over and walked into the park, surrounded by the strange, weirdly-shaped rocks.

The funeral was my ultimate destination and I had every intention of being there. I knew the park was going to take up valuable time. But then I rationalized that even if I missed the funeral mass, I could make it to the reception.

I had fond childhood memories of Uncle Ernie playing his guitar and singing Elvis Presley songs. He always seemed to be thoroughly enjoying himself when he played at our family holiday parties, and his music reverberated with energy and fun. He drew all of us in, making us want to dance and sing. Over the years, our family had celebrations for all the major Christian holidays, Memorial Day, Fourth of July, Labor Day, and many birthday and anniversary parties where he would perform.

A relative owned a bar where Uncle Ernie, his two sons, Uncle Joe, and his brother Ramon played in the family band. They played fun, lively songs to dance to, popular songs as well as some polka and Mexican songs.

I really loved being a part of our family. My mother's side had seven girls, three boys, thirty-five cousins, including myself and my sister and brother. Most of her family lived in the Denver area so there were always cousins to play with and talk to.

The fact that I never made it to the funeral or reception made me feel sad and a little guilty. Ernie's final days were wracked with diabetes, and he had to have his legs amputated. I may have only seen him once during the last ten years. I remembered he was still happy and made me feel like he genuinely liked me.

I left the Garden of the Gods Park. Listening to the Voice, I drove,
turning on various streets, not knowing where I was going. After
a few miles of turns, I ended up at Seven Falls. I had been here long
ago as a child and another time when I was married, with my ex,
Paige, and Ryan.

It was a happy time then and the memories came flooding back. I
could see us smiling, exploring the falls and walking along the trail,
ending up at Box Canyon Falls. Sometimes I really missed our
family … the way it used to be. Everything had changed so quickly.

I continued to drive into the park. The entryway was beautiful
with a canopy of trees and rocks all around. For a short period of
time, Jayne and Ted, her then-boyfriend who was now her husband, took care of me and we made a trip to the Garden of the
Gods and then drove to the entrance of Seven Falls. That was as
far as we made it. We didn't have money to pay for the entrance
fee. I remembered the disappointment and feeling that I really
hated being poor.

The South Cheyenne Canyon Road to Seven Falls had been called
"The Grandest Mile of Scenery" in Colorado.
They were located in a 1,000-foot granite
canyon. Ponderosa pine, Douglas fir, juniper, and blue spruce
were found everywhere in this majestic area of Colorado.

Why was I led here?

I parked the car and walked into the restaurant/gift shop to
buy a ticket. After paying the entrance fee, I browsed through
the clothing racks, choosing a gift for Thomas, Paige, and Ryan.
After paying for my purchases, I headed into the small café.
Perfect! I was hungry, and ordered a chili dog, fries, and a drink.

Sliding off the round stool, I walked outside looking at the steep stairs zigzagging up the mountain, skirting each of the seven waterfalls. I remembered how we encouraged Paige and Ryan to keep climbing and how proud they were when they made it to the top of the stairs.

I didn't know my purpose for being here. Why was I led here? Deciding to just go with this mystery/adventure, I climbed the stairs. I noticed the elevator was still a choice, but it felt good to get some exercise.

I followed the dirt trail, going up past the beautifully lit falls. Each of the seven falls had a colorful light that illuminated the waterfall.

I realized that I wouldn't be going to Trinidad and for whatever reason needed to be here. I walked along the trail, taking in the beauty. So far, I had not seen any other visitors. I made it to Box Canyon Falls. Remembering Paige and Ryan playing there, I breathed a deep, troubled sigh. They were the light of my life and inspired me in my darkest moments to keep living. The crash of memories left me missing the kids. I stood deep in thought, thinking back on our family.

I crossed over the small creek and climbed on top of some boulders. I was hidden up here and sitting on a flat spot on the rock where I could look down over the mountain trail I had walked up. I lay down on my back, looking up at the stormy sky. It looked like rain. Summer storms in Colorado could move fast and furiously, especially in the mountains.

I shut my eyes and prayed for understanding, to make peace with my past, for healing and guidance. I prayed for my children that things would get easier. They say time heals all wounds. I could only hope.

Feeling a warmth on my body, I opened my eyes. Looking up I saw a stream of crystal glowing light flowing down from the sky onto my body. It looked like crystal rain. Bewildered, I sat up and the flow stopped. For several minutes, my black slacks and blue top looked white, like crystal snow. As I stared in surprise, the crystal white light absorbed into my clothes and my clothes were once again normal in appearance. I closed my eyes, hoping the light would flow again. Opening my eyes, and looking up, the sky appeared normal. The crystal glowing light had disappeared.

Suddenly, a loud thunderous boom echoed in the canyon, followed by a crack of lightning, way too close for comfort. I felt as if God was talking directly to me. The thunder kept booming, moving closer and getting louder as lightning bolts filled the air with electricity.

It was time to go. I made my way off the rock, running down the trail as heavy rain poured down. I was at the top of the stairs and opted for the elevator ride down to get out of the rain. I remembered how the kids loved the glass elevator ride. The elevator dropped smoothly back to the bottom of the falls.

Walking across the parking lot, I returned to my car and climbed inside. Then I asked, "Now what?"

I did not feel like I had accomplished anything. No answers were given, although it really felt as if I had been in God's presence. And the crystal rain! I had never seen anything like it. I drove to the dumpster behind the restaurant and left an item I had bought.

Everywhere I went I had to leave something. I do not know why but that was what I was told. It was part of the Game. I left the falls not really knowing what to do next, but thinking I would drive back home.

Strange and foolish but I did as the Voice instructed.

Listening to the Voice telling me where to turn, I found myself in Manitou Springs, a charming little mountain town built and established in the 1870s. Americana vintage motels and tourist shops line the streets with restaurants, bars, and a nice park and picnic area in the middle of town.

I took a series of turns and parked off the main strip. I asked a young hippie guy if I could park next to where he was playing with a toddler. He was friendly and said, "Not a problem."

Going inside one of the shops, I was delighted to see racks of bohemian-style clothing. I chose a pair of avatar army-green flowy cotton pants with a rope belt. After paying for my purchase, I walked out, placing my cell phone on the bench outside of the shop and left. Strange and foolish, but I did as the Voice instructed. I left something again.

I drove back to the highway and headed home. Many questions were asked of me when I arrived. The phone had been ringing. My relatives were calling to ask where I was. Did something happen? Was I in an accident? Why didn't I show up for the funeral?

Of course, I could not really talk about what happened because it didn't make sense to me, and it sounded crazy. No one would understand. All I could say is I got a late start and decided to spend some time in the Springs and misplaced my phone.

Thomas was concerned and I felt bad about being untruthful, but I did not understand it myself. How could I possibly explain to him how it made any sense at all? I was happy he did not question me beyond what I told him.

Playing the Game, I called the bohemian shop. They had found the phone on the bench outside the store. We drove to Manitou Springs the next day and made a day of it by hiking at nearby Green Mountain and picking up a chicken strawberry fields salad from one of the restaurants on Main Street on the way home.

My "intentionally left behind" phone was found. Had I broken a rule to the Game?

sixteen
Reflection ...
Grandma and Grandpa

I believed this Voice I was hearing
was there to help me and guide me
on this mysterious journey.

I needed time to process what had happened and spent hours doing self-Reiki and praying for answers and guidance.

The healings were intense. I heard God's voice telling me *Sins of the Fathers.* Over and over, I heard this echo in my mind. It did not mean anything to me at the time. I could not connect any relevance in my life to this information. When I was meditating, I often thought about these words, yet my understanding remained elusive.

My family, mainly Grandma and aunts, were superstitious. We were told stories about a witch who would come and take you away if you were bad. When in the kitchen we were forewarned that the knives had to point down in the dishwasher. You do not want to point them up to God. And every time I hear an ambulance siren or pass a church, I should make the sign of the cross.

My mother said she was marked, cursed, as she had a dark two-inch hairy birthmark on her left arm. She said our family had been cursed by a gypsy group that passed through her town. When watching television, Grandma would often say that the world calamities were signs from God, and these were the end days.

Most of my family was devout Catholics. They believed in Jesus, the Trinity, Heaven, Hell, and purgatory. I had little knowledge of all the Catholic doctrines the church believed. My uncle was a former Catholic priest. When I was about eight years old, he declared that I had completed my holy communion by asking me if I believed in Jesus, that Jesus died for our sins, and if I loved Jesus.

The Reiki attunement had heightened my awareness on a spiritual level. My superstitious beliefs growing up became magnified. When meditating, praying, and doing self-Reiki, I asked in my prayers to be a channel of powerful love and healing like Jesus and Mary had been.

In a profound way, I came to believe in magic, evil spirits, the supernatural, and that my purpose here was spiritual and involved battling demons. I believed this Voice I was hearing was there to help me and guide me on this mysterious journey.

A few days later, I left again.

Once again, I was headed south toward Colorado Springs in the late spring. It was early evening, and my destination was unsure. I ended up at the Peterson Air Force Base …

11:56 was illuminated.

The North American Aerospace Defense Command known as NORAD that provides aerospace warning, air sovereignty, and protection for North America.

I pulled up to the entrance gate where Air Force guards were checking in cars. Explaining to the guard that I had not meant to go inside and had taken a wrong turn, he directed me to turn around and instructed how to get back on the highway.

That was strange, but I enjoyed the peek I had at the entrance found inside the mountain.

As I drove, the Voice gave me directions ... directions like turn right, turn left, keep driving. Urging me on with a sense of importance, I had to make it to a certain place by midnight. I drove on a rural road in the dark of night, hands clutching the wheel as I sped down the road, going past 100 mph.

My gas needle was almost in the red.

Hazel wasn't liking it. She was shaking and not taking the curves well. I felt like my hands were glued to her steering wheel. I held on tightly using quick wrist moves to keep Hazel going straight. I looked to my left as a sleek sports car passed me easily. I watched the clock, 11:56 was illuminated. Exiting off the road I drove into a small town, a town that most would miss in the blink of an eye. Whatever this Game was, I had made it.

I drove around the dozen or so small houses with tiny yards and a few mobile homes. Feeling relieved, I got back on the road driving slowly, headed back to the city, grateful I did not get a speeding ticket.

I listened to the Voice telling me where to turn. No gas station in sight, my gas needle was in the red. I ended up at Union and Pikes Peak, at Memorial Park. Parking my car, I walked to the Memorial, no clue as to what it was.

It was a memorial to the 9/11 victims and firefighters that died during the terrorists' attack. I sat and cried, remembering the horror I felt when I watched live television and the airplanes crashing into the twin towers. I was emotional and weeping, when a police officer came up and told me I had left my car unlocked and my purse on the seat. He was very kind and asked me if I was okay.

No, I was not okay …. I don't know what I was doing.

I felt like I was moving in a trance, and doing these weird things, like a puppet. Getting back into the car, I drove through an upper-class neighborhood of large homes. I would guess the average square footage to be around 5,000 square feet or larger, with long driveways, three and four car garages and immaculate yards. Again, no clue as to why I had driven there.

I passed street signs with names that called out a story, such as Hopeful Drive, Haven Circle, Harmony Drive, and Blissful Circle. And now, it was time for me to head home, or so I thought.

seventeen
Sacred Places

Now, it was time to go home.

It didn't happen … not yet.

I had to get out of Hazel and stretch my legs. And I needed to fill up on water to stop the hunger pains.

After four or five cupfuls of water, I walked around my campsite, now wet in melting snow. How I wished I could build a fire and be warm. I felt the presence of my grandparents here with me. I wasn't alone. It was freezing out here in the open and I made a quick dash back to Hazel. Glad to be out of the colder air, I sat on the passenger seat holding my knees to my chest, trying to get warm.

Trying to understand the Game, I continued to think back on the events that happened in the last month: the strange trips with Hazel. Was my excuse that I was seeking answers to the puzzle?

As I drove along the interstate, the Voice began telling me where to turn, leading me to the US Air Force Academy. I did not want to go there because I needed gas. The Voice urged me on, to keep driving the twisty road. All I could think was, "I'm going to run out of gas." But I made it to the chapel.

Parking in the lot, I felt so relieved.

Excited and curious, I walked into the chapel and with reverence
thought of the many brave young men and women cadets and their
families that had been here before me. It felt like a sacred space.

I have a deep love for our country and our troops. After high school,
I tried to enlist in the Air Force but was disqualified because I had
a torn meniscus in my knee that was never repaired.

I was enjoying the places I had visited; just wish I knew why.

The Cadet Chapel was the most recognizable building at the
US Air Force Academy and the most visited man-made tourist
attraction in Colorado. The aluminum, glass, and steel structure
featured 17 spires that shoot 150 feet into the sky. It was considered among the most beautiful examples of modern American
academic architecture.

One of the things I loved about it is that it was an all-faith center
of worship for cadets. There were chapels within the Cadet Chapel
—Protestant, Catholic, Jewish and
What are you doing Kelly?" Buddhist, an All-Faiths Room, and
a Falcon Circle. Each had its own entrance.

I walked around looking up at the beautiful spires. Inside the
chapel, I sat in one of the pews and said a prayer for my children,
Thomas, the USA and our troops, and myself for help, guidance,
protection, and enlightenment.

Now, it was time to go home. I needed to go home. Worried I
could not make it to a gas station; that decision was taken out of
my hands when I turned the key to the ignition and the engine

didn't respond. I was out of gas. I approached a woman and asked her if she had a phone I could borrow, that I needed to make an emergency call. She was happy to help, and finally, I phoned home.

Thomas answered. "What are you doing, Kelly?"

I told him my predicament, where I was, and that I needed help. He was unbelievably nice about it. "Why didn't you stop and get gas?" was said more than once.

I felt foolish that I had planned so poorly, so caught up in the Game, and eager to get to my destination that I didn't gas up. I apologized to him for asking him to help me out and having to make the long drive from Denver. When I heard him say, "Okay, I'll be there as quick as possible and bring gas," it left me with the ultimate feeling of gratitude.

He seemed to accept me just as I am.

What was going on with me was so confusing. I didn't understand it. How could I expect him to?

Thomas was my savior, my rock, and I was so grateful for our relationship, our love, the little family we had, the life we shared, along with his kindness and support. He seemed to accept me just as I was, not judging me for making poor decisions, which I seemed to be doing more of.

I waited a few hours and Thomas showed up as promised, with a full gas can. I happily followed him back home, not sharing where I had been or my thoughts.

He never asked.

eighteen

My Cornerstones ...

His words would echo in my mind,
motivating me to work or get busy with chores.

Grateful for the distraction from my racing thoughts, I picked
up the box of pictures from the back seat. I could not help but
think nothing was a coincidence and the photos played a part in
my quest for answers to the questions that I kept asking myself.

Looking at a snapshot of my grandparents, I reminisced about
the time I spent at their house and Grandma's homemade food.
Every Sunday she would prepare a beef roast with rolls, potatoes,
green beans, and chocolate cake. Anyone in our family was always
welcome to come over and have supper.

Grandma was an excellent cook, and so quick and efficient in
providing meals for her large family. The meals she made were
simple yet so satisfying. I loved her homemade tortillas, beans,
chili, tostados, calibecitos (succotash) hamburger/potato soup,
lentils, pork chops, spaghetti, fried chicken, and oatmeal cake.
There was oatmeal or cereal for breakfast or occasionally fried
eggs, bacon, and toast. As my memories brought up her many
delicious meals, my stomach grumbled in hunger.

The celebration of Grandma and Grandpa's 50th wedding
anniversary photo was in my hands. They were dancing in a
polka line, smiling, and looking happy. Grandpa was a good

father, husband, grandfather, and a devout Catholic. When he lived in the San Luis Valley, he was a practicing Penitente and a member of the Los Hermanos Penitente, a semi-secret society of Roman Catholics in the American Southwest. It was well-known for its extreme practice of penance, in an effort to make reparation for one's sins.

The practice centered on various forms of body-mortification,

Always work hard and don't be lazy.

especially flagellation, whipping themselves with cords, and culminated annually in a ritual reenactment of the crucifixion of Jesus Christ. Almost all members of the group lived in southern Colorado or northern New Mexico.

Grandpa had the best work ethic and was the hardest worker I have ever known. He never missed a day of work in his 30 years at the railroad until he retired. They had ten children. When Grandma went into labor, he would drop her off at the hospital and go to work.

He would often say to me, "Hita, you need to always work hard and don't be lazy." He would make a phone call every morning to my home and to other family members, to wake them up for work or school. The phone would ring until you answered, and he would always say, "Are you up? Get up out of bed! Time to get to work!"

My response was always the same. "Yes, Grandpa, I'm up, just putting my feet on the ground." He really loved these daily calls to us until old age and dementia took him from us.

It was a nice way to start the day. Thanking him, I would say, "It's such a good thing you called because I was sound asleep." I would tell him a few things I was going to do that day and hung up with, "I love you."

Grandpa was the only stable father figure I had in my life and his words stuck with me, although I will admit there were times when I was lazy, or to be more precise ...

He loved to tell stories.

low energy. His words would echo in my mind, motivating me to work or get busy with chores. Because of him, I tried to do my best and work hard, no matter what I was doing: a job, cleaning, or whatever else. But I did like my downtime and was guilty of procrastinating at times.

My early memories of him was his laughing and bright brown eyes as he pushed his false teeth out of his mouth at me. I thought it was funny and he got such a kick out of teasing his grandkids with his skill in repositioning his teeth with a flick of his tongue. When I visited, he was always at the front door to greet me with a quarter in his hand to give to me. I loved it! When I was a child, a quarter could buy a lot of candy. Everyone got a quarter and an orange marshmallow circus peanut. As much as I loved candy and sweets, I did not like the orange chewy peanut, and always politely declined.

Grandma was always patient and nice, somewhat quiet and demure but a calming presence. She provided childcare for me, Jayne, and Roger when I was a baby and toddler. As I got older and went to school, I didn't see them as much. Often the two would speak in Spanish, when they did not want us to know what they were saying and when she would scold Grandpa for various things. Sometimes he was silly and loved to joke and she would tell him, "Callate," meaning "be quiet."

Grandpa would just laugh. He was always happy, but you did not dare cross him or be disrespectful in his presence. He was quick to take off his belt and hit you with it. Usually just the threat was enough, and we quickly did as he said.

He loved to tell stories about growing up and living in the San Luis Valley. He had loved being a sheepherder and farmer and growing his own food. When they moved to Denver, he always had a large garden and enjoyed giving away the vegetables he had grown.

In the picture I was holding, Grandma had her bright red hair in a 1950s-style beehive. She was petite, about five feet tall, with blue-gray eyes and had an elegant, subdued air about her. Her hair was always carefully styled, and she dressed nicely in slacks or a dress. Going to daily Mass was a part of her routine. She rarely missed it and I remember her rosary beads were often in her hands.

Looking at the pictures made me feel less alone.

Whenever she babysat me, she took me to Spanish mass with her. I could not understand anything the priest said, but I did memorize most of the prayer responses. She always had a piece of Wrigley's Juicy Fruit gum to give me if I promised to be quiet and did not let anyone see me chewing it.

Before her death, she lived with her daughter Vera. When I visited her at my Aunt Vera's house, she was close to passing. She was at peace and her face glowed as if she was looking at a beautiful sight. Grandma appeared to be very happy. That look on her face gave me hope and faith. She surely was deserving of Heaven.

I really missed her. It seemed like all the fun left our family when she passed from the early onset of Alzheimer's disease.

Looking at the pictures made me feel less alone. I felt like Grandma and Grandpa and Aunt Lucy were there in spirit with me as the blizzard dropped snow outside.

 Lifesaving Trivia

Day three dawned and the sun rose shining in a clear blue sky. The snowstorm was over.

The snow was blowing sideways. I could not see beyond the car hood. It was bitterly cold. I curled into a ball, again, hugging my knees to my chest, trying keep warm. Thinking about Grandma and her cooking had increased my hunger. Now, my empty stomach was all I could think about.

Putting down the pictures, I read more of *The Worst-Case Scenario Survival Game* cards. I learned that if you want to inform searchers of the direction you went, you should make an arrow with rocks or sticks. Another great tip was to put a small stone in your mouth if you are dehydrated, and your mouth will produce saliva.

Little did I know I would be using those tips within a day. It filled my time reading the cards, but most of the scenarios did not apply to my situation. There were tips on how to cure furs, how to stop a baby from crying, or how to remove a gag. They were amusing in some cases, but totally irrelevant.

Huddled in the car, the snow fell as if it would never end. Looking out the driver's side window, I could see that the creek had risen at least four inches. I was not too worried that it would seep into the car, at least not yet.

There was no possibility of making a fire for warmth if I ventured from the car. Everything around me was soaked. I had to pee. I remember reading in one of the hiking guides that Thomas and I carried in our backpacks: *Walk at least 20 feet from any creek water.*

I made a quick exit from the car, wading into the creek water, I walked my 20 steps and squatted. I carried the cover to the transistor radio and made it into a cup. Filling it with fresh creek water, I drank from it to the point I was almost over-drinking.

The coming darkness filled me with dread.

I was dehydrated and the cold water was refreshing. Once full, I felt better.

It was dusk and I felt hopeless. The coming darkness filled me with dread. The same worries raced through my head about my situation, and I worried about my children and Thomas. Everyone must be so concerned and confused by my absence. I certainly was. How I wished I was home.

Day three dawned and the sun rose shining in a clear blue sky. The snowstorm was over. I opened the door and emptied the bottle of urine that I filled from all the creek water I had drunk. Squirming in my seat with the strong urge to pee, I positioned myself over the bottle and controlled the steady stream that steamed in the frozen air.

I decided I would wait until it warmed up outside before I ventured out to pee again … and to fill myself with fresh water. The creek's stream was flowing fast and just under the edge of the floorboards. At least Hazel was not flooded.

Waiting in the car was difficult. All I had were my memories and regrets that I may not be able to tell my kids and Thomas how much I loved them all. I knew that he would handle the situation at home and provide some comfort and support for the kids. I was trying to stay positive.

I picked up the box of photos again and sifted through them, turning my attention to an old photo, maybe 50 years old, of two relatives who were standing in front of a large painting of the *Angelus.* In Millet's famous painting, a peasant boy and girl in France recite the Angelus at dark. The prayer originated during the time of the Crusades as a prayer for peace and tranquility for their country. I was amazed at the old photo. They stood with their heads bowed in prayer and toward the portrait as if encouraging the viewer to pray.

Grandma and Aunt Lucy's family were Spaniards who fled Spain and Portugal during the Spanish Inquisition. They were Sephardic, Crypto Jews/Conversos. Aunt Vera, and her husband, Al, who taught sociology and ethnic studies, had researched our family history and genealogy.

Our ancestors had traveled from the Iberian Coast up through the Gulf of Mexico around 1570 and headed north, settling in northern New Mexico and then later moved to the San Luis Valley around the year 1700. The area later became part of the state of Colorado, which would officially become a state in 1876. My children were the 15th generation removed from Europe.

Our family had a small ranch where they herded sheep, living off the land and food they grew, sometimes bartering for supplies and services. My great grandmother was a *curandera*, Spanish for a female folk healer. A medicine woman who uses herbs or psychoactive plants, magic, and spiritualism to treat illness, induce visions, impart traditional wisdom, etc., a female shaman.

When my mother was seven, she became ill with polio. Grandma thought she had a bad spirit in her. She could not stand or walk and was becoming paralyzed very quickly. She and my great-grandmother knew nothing about polio at that time. Earlier that day she had gone on a horse ride and picnic in the woods with her sisters. When they returned home, Mom's sister, Vera, said she saw a tick on her sister Sally's neck. They tried pulling out the little bug but had to dig it out of the flesh with a hot needle.

> What was put on a tray each day was alien.

Great-grandmother tried to cleanse her, and they prayed for little Sally. Nothing helped and she rapidly became worse. She was laid in the back of a truck on a bed of hay for the 263-mile trip to Denver, where she was admitted at Mercy Hospital.

Mom once told me she remembered being confused and scared. She did not understand what was happening and was put in isolation. She spoke only Spanish and did not understand the doctors or nurses that helped her. Not liking the food, she refused to eat, losing even more weight. The hospital didn't serve fresh meat, potatoes, homemade breads, tortillas, and beans. What was put on a tray each day was alien to her.

The polio changed her life in dramatic ways. Polio stunted the growth of her leg by two inches and eliminated much of the muscle that would be expected on a normal leg. She was disabled and walked with a limp most of her life. It wasn't until she was 60 that she finally got proper shoes with a built-up sole.

She believed her long hospital experience had made her detached from others and cold in expressing any feelings. The isolation from her family had made her where she could not express affection. She missed her family, and their visits were few during her three months of isolation.

Putting the pictures aside, I thought about how scary that must have been for her and thought of my own regrettable solitude.

I prayed and did Reiki on myself, sending Paige and Ryan distant healing. My finger felt and looked better. The gash was now shallow and the redness and swelling were gone. The cuts and scrapes on my legs and arms now looked like they were healing.

I prayed and asked myself over and over … *why?*

Why did I get stranded here?

Why did you lead me here? Am I going to die here?

I did not hear answers to my questions, but I did sense that I would be okay. My mind relived how my foot had suddenly pushed on the gas pedal landing me in the ditch. It had moved as if someone else controlled my body. That was my life lately: the Voice leading me on, like a marionette.

Who was this Voice that filled my head?

Was this a friend or should I be alarmed?

As my eyes took in the pictures that I had my hands kept reaching for, I realized they were a special gift. My family was with me, bringing back and resurrecting memories from long ago. It was a special gift … but they made me even more aware of how far away I was from them. And how alone I was.

The snow was melting fast, and the car was warming up inside. Anything was better than the freezing cold of the last few nights. I stayed huddled in the car, berating myself for making the many stupid mistakes that had plagued me.

Eventually, I got out of the car. The creek water was receding and thankfully was a few inches below the running board now. Wading through the creek I climbed up the embankment and surveyed my previous fire, now a pile of ash. Another fire was impossible. All the wood was soaked.

Foremost in my mind was something to drink and eat. The creek water was refreshing. Was it clean and okay to drink? The answer was … it did not matter. It was all I had. I drank from the small plastic radio cover, filling it up over and over, drinking to slake my thirst as well as curb my hunger pangs.

If only I could find something edible to eat. Looking around, I surveyed the landscape, desperate for anything to fill my belly.

There is no hope of finding food here. Finding some green grass surfacing through the thawing snow, I pulled a handful and put it in my mouth. Chewing and chewing, the grass did not break down where I could swallow it. It tasted bitter and awful. I tried grinding my teeth sideways. Finally, I spit it out.

There was nothing here to eat. I did not think about insects that could probably be dug up. It didn't even come to mind, maybe because the thought was so repulsive.

I walked away from the creek and squatted to pee. No urge for a bowel movement, probably the stress, and what was there to move? I had not eaten for more than two days.

Being hungry wasn't a stranger to me. I remember my stomach hurting as a child and searching for food in empty cupboards. But even then, I knew Mom just needed to go grocery shop and soon I would eat again.

I told myself that I could mentally deal with the lack of food if I think of it as a fast. I've fasted on liquids in the past, but food was available. It was a choice then and I could quit the fast whenever I wanted. This fast would be like nothing I've ever experienced.

I felt ravenous; I was starving. This empty hunger was something I had never known before.

All I could think was … *there is no hope of finding food here.*

twenty
Leaving My Shelter

*I felt restless, helpless,
and hated that I was stuck in this car.*

I was thankful that Hazel wasn't a car without options. The seats in the front had lots of flexibility. I reclined the passenger seat back and curled up, taking a nap.

When I awoke, it was dark outside. I had no idea what time it was. It felt like I slept for four or five hours. My sleep the previous nights were troubled and light, often waking up and listening to sounds outside. I still felt I was being watched … that there was "something" out there. Was it my imagination … or was it my intuition? I felt I was being chased and I felt so vulnerable here by myself … stranded. My mind was telling me that there was a "something," I just didn't know what it was.

I turned on my little radio, searching for other stations but could only tune into the country station. The announcer talked about the storm and snowfall amounts. He sounded cheery. I wished I had something to be cheery about. I felt restless, helpless, and hated that I was stuck in this car. After some time, I crawled to the back seat of Hazel and slept … again.

DAY FOUR

Morning finally came after another choppy night of sleeping. I awoke to brightness and freezing air. The steam from my breath was coming out in little puffs. I felt achy and stiff from the frigid cold.

This was so alien to my normal life, all the people and comforts of my home I took for granted. I had hit my low point and thinking of my dire situation, I began to play out in my mind the possible scenarios of how this would all end. I felt I was doomed.

My family surely was concerned at my absence and probably had called the police by now. My mother must know by now and, therefore, my aunts, uncles, and cousins. It didn't matter. They would never find me here. I fell into complete despair. I hadn't heard any voices, cars, or ATVs since the first night before the blizzard hit.

Dreading the thought of getting out of Hazel, I had no choice but to open the passenger door and wade through the creek so I could go to my pee spot. The water had receded a few more inches. Relieving myself, my breath freezing in the frozen air, I hurried back to Hazel, where it was not much warmer. I had a sickening feeling that if I continued to just sit in this car, I would not be found, or if I were, I would be found dead.

I was doomed if I stayed here much longer.

Picking up the box of pictures to look at again, I could not imagine having so many children. How did they manage with their limited money?

Grandma and Grandpa had been successful in raising their
ten children. Their values were old-fashioned: they only spent
money on what was necessary. They weren't consumers unless
needed and their frugalness supported their ten children. In the
present world, it would be difficult to survive in with such a large
family unless being money-conscious was part of everyday living.

Looking at the pictures of my extended family made me miss my
children, Thomas, and my dogs. I would be so grateful for a chance
to hug them all once more. I realized now, too
late maybe, how much I had to be grateful
for. We were not a perfect family. Sometimes
there were arguments and misunderstandings, especially lately
since we moved into the rental. But I know we loved each other.
I wished I had the chance to love them again ... to be with them
again. I would love them unconditionally.

The Voice was telling me that I had to seek help. I wanted to sit
in the car and wait for a miracle of someone finding me. I did not
want to go anywhere. I knew that it was unwise to leave a car if
stranded from a variety of resources over the years. But the Voice
was persistent. I heard, *You can't stay here.* I argued in my head,
saying, *Why? I'm safe and have shelter and water.*

Feeling antsy and compelled by the urging Voice, I began to gather
up my purse with my wallet along with a few of the family photos,
the transistor radio and lighter. I locked the car and dropped the
keys inside my purse. I was wearing all the clothing I had, and my
flip-flops with a two-inch wedge sole.

The Worst-Case Scenario Survival Game was on my mind. I remembered one of the tips and made an arrow on the ground with rocks, pointing south, the direction I was headed.

My intention was to walk back out on the road to the 7-11 convenience store. I figured it was about 15 miles, something I should be able to do. I tied the silver space blanket onto the car, thinking it would help Hazel be spotted. The finder would run the license plate and maybe find that I was missing and start searching for me. I do not know if that was the wise thing to do. I might need it, but it sure did not generate any warmth when I had it, and it should be fairly easy to see from above.

I figured that I wasn't far from the road I had driven on and could walk back to the store. I was guessing it would take me all day.

Drinking more capfuls of the cold creek water and knowing I had a plan, I felt energized. I started walking south on the road parallel to the creek. The ground was squishy with thick mud that was three to four inches deep and hard to walk on in my flip flops. My feet were sliding off the sides when I stepped onto the soft, uneven ground so I decided to walk barefoot.

The sun was shining, bright and warm. The snow was gone, and in its wake was the deep mud and drenched ground. I stopped, looking back at Hazel with her silver banner blowing in the breeze. With sadness and worry, I left my shelter, hopeful that I would arrive at the 7-11 by the end of the day.

At least I was making moves.

It did not seem impossible to walk the distance to the store, I told myself. I remembered Thomas's words of encouragement on earlier hikes and it motivated me. Just take one step in front of another and I will get there eventually. Maybe I would see someone and flag them down. I felt optimistic. At least I was making moves, *doing* something to help myself.

I stopped and filled the little cup over and over, drinking water, and continued walking. The dirt road I had driven four days ago looked unpassable in a car; maybe a 4-wheeler could make it. I enjoyed the feel of the soft cold mud under my feet and how it squished between my toes as I walked.

I had not walked very far when I came to a fork in the road. A path branched off to the left of the road I had been walking on, or I could stay to the right on the road. Just in front of the fork was a large tree that had fallen and was blocking the road. I looked for a way around it but further down the road was more fallen trees. It appeared that the small path to the left was higher, not as muddy, and followed the creek and the road. I called to mind a hike with Thomas, where he sang the lyrics derived from the poem "The Bonnie Banks of Loch Lomond." Do I "take the high road" or the "low road," portions of a verse from the poem, now a highly recognized song. I decided to take the "high road" and veered off to the left.

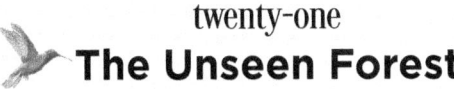

twenty-one
The Unseen Forest

*I was blindly walking in the forest,
away from the road.*

I could not believe my luck! On the east side of the road, I spotted a house, and cars parked in front of it. Walking up the hill, away from the path, I could see it half hidden in the trees. As I walked in the direction of the house, I looked down to carefully step over the forest brush and vegetation in my bare feet. When I looked up, I had lost sight of it.

Where did it go?

I continued walking up the hill, excited to find help. I continued east, believing I was getting closer, but the house was gone. Was it a mirage? I know I had seen the house very clearly and Jeeps parked in front of it.

Had I bypassed it?

Somehow, I missed it. Confused, I looked back down the hill. The ground where I was standing was not as wet and the pine needles were soft under my bruised cold feet. I was compelled to keep walking, still looking for the house and grateful to be out of the mud, holding out hope that help was nearby.

I made it to the top of a hill. The house was nowhere in sight. There was nothing there. Rocky terrain surrounded me with large boulders and pine trees. Noticing a small movement, just the slightest motion up ahead, I froze. Watching for more movement, I saw a baby deer, a fawn, move its head and look directly at me.

I was so relieved, sighing out my held breath. I moved closer to see if it was hurt. I approached slowly, not wanting to scare the frightened fawn. The poor baby was shaking, trembling in fear, probably fear of me. Maybe ten feet away, I could see the fawn was scared. Her soft brown eyes stared at me. She was beautiful with light brown fur and white spots, maybe a month old. She looked so fragile, and I wondered if she could walk.

In some native american legends, deer is a totem or symbol of gentleness. There is a story of a little deer that with kindness overcame the anger and mean spirit of a demon that prevented the connection of man with the Great Spirit. With deer's loving kindheartedness she healed the heart of the demon bringing peace for all of mankind. Humanity didn't need to feel fear anymore, the path was made clear.

For a few minutes I forgot about my own problems. I wanted to pet her and comfort her but thought it might scare the mother if she smelled my scent on her baby and then she might be abandoned. I felt like this shaking little creature was a mirror of me and my own vulnerability and fear of the unknown.

I silently thanked the little fawn for her presence and started making my way across the mountain, turning to the south once again.

I slowly made my way through the forest, the brief joy quickly fading away. I had made a bad move in walking away from my water source and Hazel, and now I was deep in the forest, completely alone and lost. I continued with painstaking effort, taking care to step over rocks and tree limbs.

I was deep in the forest, completely alone and lost.

This was not a path. I was blindly walking in the forest, away from the road. Yet, the Voice was there, telling me I would be okay, to keep moving forward. Despite my reservations of listening, I moved forward, thinking I would continue south and head back west to the road. The Voice was loud in my mind. I must continue and trust it and I would be okay.

I loved the forest, with the smell of the pine trees and juniper berries, and the freshness of the air. It gave me energy and I felt a deep connection, maybe a memory of another life lived where I was at home in nature.

My thirst was intense; my tongue felt swollen and dry. Finding a small pebble, I placed it under my tongue, one of the survival game answers. I did feel my mouth creating moisture. It worked!

I made it to a road and began walking, thinking of the song I heard earlier about a man in his pickup truck that came to his love's rescue on an old dirt road. I imagined Thomas in a truck driving alongside me, rescuing me. Of course, it was wishful thinking.

A few hundred feet ahead of me, I noticed a movement and saw a mountain lion sitting on top of some boulders. I stopped, frozen with fear. The Voice came into my mind and told me that I would not be attacked. I slowly started to back up, keeping my eyes on the lion.

Majestic, beautiful, his tail swished back and forth, so large. The cinnamon color of its coat with patches of white fur helped him **My fear began to subside.** to blend into the rock he was sitting upon. He was massive and watched my every move. I was surprised that the lion was so big. Easily as large as the big lions I saw at the Denver Zoo. It could close the distance between us and take me down in a matter of seconds.

My fear began to subside, my racing heart slowed, as it appeared the lion was not interested in my presence. I had a mental impression that it was allowing me to pass. I did not do all the things I was supposed to do, like waving my arms and making noise. Instead, I continued to silently back away.

The quiet, observant king of the forest continued to recline on his rock. I was feeling very lucky that I was spared.

I felt exposed, and easy prey for this huge cat to kill. I was power-less in this moment, shocked to be looking into the face of this amazing feline. It was terrifying to be completely at its mercy.

In my mind I thought of the courageous lion from the *Wizard of OZ* and wondered what message this lion was bringing me. I knew the appearance of this powerful totem was courage, strength and agility. I didn't feel very agille, my feet felt numb, bruised and frozen.

I was just grateful that I was still alive, and that I was allowed to continue on my way. The lion continued to watch me as I made a wide berth between us. Letting out my held-in breath, I started to breathe normally, but I knew that the lion could easily find me and attack if it chose. I heard the Voice telling me I was safe. The Voice had been right.

twenty-two
The Promise

I knew if I got out of this mess it would be a miracle.

My preoccupation with watching the lion had led me back into the forest. I walked for a while, putting distance between myself and the lion, praying for intercession and guidance. The Voice made its presence known again. It told me to follow twos. I was to be led by numbers.

I knew that everything was energy and had a vibration. I looked for twos, two of anything: a tree where the trunk was split in two; a plant with two flowers; anything that revealed to me that it was a twosome. I know, I know … it sounds crazy, but that was the direction I went, following the twos. It took me in a southernly direction.

The Law of Vibration revealed everything was energy through Quantum Physics, the Unified Field or Matrix. And two was the number of Eve, the first woman. I felt that I had been given a compass. My belief was that these signs and numbers were guidance for me to follow and eventually to be found. In ancient times, the number two symbolized the mother and female principle, the symbol of creative development, also struggle, movement, and effort.

The dualism of the two signifies wisdom, reason, and intuition. It worked for me.

Numbers had become important after I earned the Master level of Reiki. I recently learned about numerology and the influence numbers play in our everyday lives. My life path or destiny number is seven. People with this life path characteristic tend to be spiritual, intuitive, intellectual and sometimes loners that may seem mysterious.

Since my attunement, I clearly understood that my life's purpose was spiritual. I could cast off the old ties to the material world and focus on my quest for self-knowledge and wisdom. The Voice was clearly telling me to follow the number two. I scouted for anything around me that would be symbolic of the union of the two.

I listened and was led. Eventually, I found myself at a dam. Not a soul to be seen anywhere nor a critter—two-legged, four-legged, or winged. I was unable to access the water and felt the need to keep moving. While climbing down a steep embankment of a quarry of rocks, I needed both hands to help me scoot down on my butt.

Tying my sandals to the strings of my lime green Patagonia windbreaker, they hung on each side of my chest. I made it to the bottom of the rocks but found I had lost both of my flip-flops, but my purse was still slung over my shoulder. Looking back up, I realized there was no way I could traverse the 100+ foot height. Anyway, I was clueless as to where my flip-flops had detached from my jacket strings.

I was cold ... and miserable at the bottom of a quarry.

It was late afternoon and soon it would be dark. There was no shelter in sight. My senses told me that I needed to stop and make a fire. I was cold ... and miserable at the bottom of a quarry.

My internal dialogue kicked in.

> *You have made so many stupid mistakes, so many*
> *huge mistakes.*
>
> *Everything you've done is against what you and*
> *Thomas knew and practiced when you hiked together.*
>
> *What were you thinking when you left Hazel?*
>
> *You've made a mess of everything.*

I lay on the ground, exhausted and hungry, and thinking about the fact that I had stopped taking my medications five days before I set out with Hazel. Could it be the reason why I was feeling so confused?

I was an expert at berating myself. And I knew if I got out of this mess, it would be a miracle.

The feeling of being watched was even more intense. Clearly there were large predators in the forest, like the mountain lion, bears, and coyotes. I was helpless to defend myself if any attacked me. And an attacker wouldn't be human if there was one.

My walk had slowed to a snail's pace. But the Voice surfaced again, assuring me that I would be okay, just keep moving. When I heard this in my head, I felt that the Great Spirit was talking to me … that it was with me.

My inner thoughts welcomed that assurance. At this point, my weaknesses were becoming more pronounced. I was physically depleted, barely able to stand. If a fight surfaced in anyway, I would be down quickly.

Throughout the day, prayer was my constant companion. I prayed to God, asking Jesus to help me; to give me a second chance to be with my family again.

I stood, unsteady, lightheaded, looking up at the sky and spoke to the Great Spirit. I believed the Voice I was now hearing was speaking back to my prayers. I heard questions that asked me if I would help humanity through my ordeal. With full voice, I always answered, "Yes," at least during those first few days.

I felt myself falling backward; my vision was weird.

I promised I would do whatever was asked if I was saved. The Voice replied, *"You will be helped if you allow your story to be used to help humanity."*

I made a pledge right then that I would do whatever it took to atone for my life if I got a second chance. As I looked up at the sky, I expected a response. There was nothing … and suddenly, I felt myself falling backward, into a depression in the forest floor that was overgrown with dead grass, my vision was weird like still frames and a pronounced hesitancy like a computerized eyeball in freeze-frame. As I fell, I hit my head on the ground and blacked out.

When I regained consciousness, I was lying flat on my back on the forest floor staring at the darkening sky and trees surrounding me. Slowly sitting up, the Voice was there.

Why do you want to live?

Was this the Great Spirit speaking to me? I thought of Paige, Ryan, Thomas, Kristiana, and all my relatives. Each were precious lives that I loved. Of course, my two beloved boxers were in the mix. There were so many other reasons that I cared about just living … and now, surviving.

I never believed that God knew me. The idea seemed so impossible. I prayed a lot … and I was fully aware that there was a God and my entire life was known. The good I've done and received. And there's the bad … times I've made too many bad decisions in the past. The thoughts that were rolling around in my head were overwhelming.

Immediately, I felt shame and regret. I knew I had sinned and now realized that I had a price to pay for my past mistakes. Was this it … this troubling situation I'm in? God had always been there watching; nothing was secret or hidden. Overcoming my fear by my desire to live, and for a higher purpose, I agreed to do whatever was asked of me.

The Voice told me that my sacrifice would save many people and God would be pleased. I could not imagine anything I could do right now would make a difference. **This felt like a darker one.** But then and there, I made a promise to be a presence for humanity by sharing my story. Hopefully, it will be one I can keep.

What would the message be?

As I lay there, the word sacrifice entered my head. When I thought about sacrifice, it brought to my mind our beloved US Military men and women. Those who serve and have served, giving their lives for our freedoms. To me, they are the true heroes. Thinking of them gave me courage.

I committed myself to do His will, offering my life to save my children, Thomas, Kristiana, my extended family, to help humanity, and for a greater cause ... for Jesus.

As I forced myself to my feet, I felt unsteady, weak, and dehydrated. But I gathered my purse and continued to walk slowly and carefully over the rocky forest ground, following "twos" and wondering about my fate. I had a newfound fear of God, as my steps moved me forward. My life had been so difficult, traumatic, and there were times I had been down a dark road. This felt like a darker one.

I was so focused on placing my feet where I wouldn't fall, I had not felt the warmth between my legs. Looking down, a streak of blood had appeared on my thighs.

There was nothing I could do but bleed.

Oh shit! *How could this be?* My period had started. The blood dripped down my legs and pooled at my feet. I had nothing to stop the flow.

I really felt like prey now ... so vulnerable, so helpless. I was scared that an animal would smell my blood. There was nothing I could do but bleed. The wetness was uncomfortable; I was a bloody mess.

This was every girl and woman's nightmare to have her period out in the middle of nowhere without hygiene supplies and I was bleeding profusely. With every step I took, blood would run down my legs, leaving a bloody trail.

Daylight was fading fast. The forest of aspen trees stood out in the dark, the white bark looking eerie with ghostly apparitions of eyes of knotted bark staring at me. I decided to sit on the ground and try to build a fire. What I needed was a torch or an isolated piece of wood that I could ignite.

I was not thinking long-term. What possessed me to take off my T-shirt and wrap it around the end of a stick, I don't know. But I did it.

Lighting the shirt on fire with my lighter, it burned fast and bright ... too fast. For a few minutes, I felt empowered while it burned. Instant warmth and my immediate surroundings were illuminated. And then, as fast as the shirt ignited, it fizzled out.

I thought the stick would catch fire as soon as the flames appeared. It didn't ... the burn was just too short. Next, I removed my bra and wrapped it around the stick, clicked the lighter to ignite my torch-to-be. Again, it burned, not so bright this time. It mostly melted on the stick, then fizzled out quickly ... another really bad decision. My makeshift torches became the torches that never were.

While sitting on the ground, I felt around me and my hand discovered a small pile of leaves and sticks. Scrunching them together, my lighter clicked one more time. The leaves burned quickly and the small flames vanished. Clicking the lighter over and over, the lighter would no longer light.

All I had left were my shorts that were dripping with blood, a lightweight jacket, and a windbreaker. Maybe it was good that the lighter fluid was gone. I might have burned everything that night.

Alone in the dark once again, my eyes strained to see more than shadows and silhouettes. In the heavily wooded forest, the treetops obscured the sky. I could only see a small part of the sky and its brilliant stars.

twenty-three
Taken Away

*The whip cracked in the air
seconds before it pierced my flesh.*

I was frightened as I sat in the pitch-black night. I had the strong feeling again that I was prey, being watched by something out there.

Slowly, I rose, unable to see more than the shadowy shapes of rocks and trees.

My heart was pounding, and I was holding my breath in fear. I saw silhouettes moving toward me. I tried to scream but had no voice and turned to run. Tripping over tree limbs, I fell and felt hands grabbing me. I blacked out.

DAYS FIVE, SIX, SEVEN

I awoke in a pit, not knowing how long I had been there or how I got there. It was like a dungeon: clammy and cold; dark with a terrible stench. Locked in a small round cell, there were rodents and bugs crawling everywhere, running over my legs and body. I could hear screaming and wailing voices, people crying out in pain. Terrified, I hit the rats, kicking them with my feet, swiping at the insects crawling on my body.

I passed out again.

When I gained consciousness, I had been placed in the back of a wagon being pulled by a horse and was traveling in dark tunnels. The screams were growing louder as I was propelled forward.

In shock and horror, I saw that I was next to a big lake of water lit with flames, and inside were throngs of people crying in agony trying to get out of the burning pool of water. As they got close to the edge, they were hit by big clubs held in the hands of monstrous demons that appeared to be at least seven feet tall.

They were grotesque-looking monsters with glowing red eyes and sharklike teeth. What blood I had left in me ran cold. It was worse than what I had seen in horror movies because they were real. It seemed to be a never-ending struggle, the poor souls reaching out their arms, trying to escape and beaten back down by demons.

Hell ... I realized I was in Hell, heavy with the sulfuric smell of rotten eggs, the air was thick and putrid.

All around me humans were being tortured with no possible escape. Men and women were being raped and sodomized over and over by the giant demons as they cried in pain, tortured over and over again. Was this to be my fate? Was I next in line?

Then I passed out again.

The next time I awoke, my arms, legs, and torso were tied down to a large rectangular-shaped flat board. I couldn't move my head; I could only look forward.

In front of me was a large white movie screen, filling an entire wall. The room was lit in fluorescent lights that glared. I hated the lights; I hated being here. I didn't want to be here. My mind reeled in shock at all that was happening to me.

Images of me and video clips of my life were played on the movie screen, starting as a child and fast forwarding to being a teen and adult. Things I thought only I knew about; private things were pouring forth. It was agony to watch myself, not able to turn my head away. I **My mouth was gagged.** looked guilty and I was terrified I would be taken to the Lake of Fire. Times that I had sinned were replayed in a never-ending loop. I was forced to watch my life unfold before me.

I could not see who, or what, was behind me and then I felt it ... the first searing pain of a whip lashed against my back. My body flinched at the pain, pulling at the ties that held me down, unable to get away from the whipping. My mouth was gagged, unable to scream at the hot pain that was building in my back.

Flashing pictures of my loved ones were interwoven in the movie of me. I felt regret, sadness, and fear. What was going to happen to me? Clearly, I had committed sin, made mistakes in my life. The whip cracked in the air seconds before it pierced my flesh. Over and over, the beating continued, the big screen with my life history played on and on. With each sin exposed, the whip lashed my back.

I didn't understand why this reel of hate was being pushed at me. I knew I was a decent, good person. Yes, I had made some mistakes, but my life was not just sin. My heart was loving, caring, generous, and compassionate.

Watching this didn't change that, I told myself. I thought if God knows everything, surely he knows the redeeming good things about me. I prayed in earnest to Jesus, to help me and forgive my sins.

Please God, Jesus, help me. Forgive me my sins, save me from this hell.

I was whipped until my skin ripped apart.

I prayed in a loop in my mind. Yes, that was where I was, in the eternal pit of Gehenna—the dark place of Hell. A place I never believed existed, what I thought was a myth meant to scare me into being a better person.

I was in shock and terrified at what I had seen and the beating I was receiving. The movie clips continued playing, and I was whipped until my skin ripped apart.

Unable to breathe, my pain was so intense. I gagged, choking and suffocating myself.

I had fallen into my own worst nightmare.

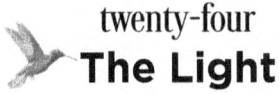

twenty-four
The Light

As I watched, I felt like
I was in the midst of a zombie movie.

I was now in a wormhole. I had a sensation of being pulled through a vortex. It felt as if I was going at warp speed through a portal of brilliant light. Before me was a beautiful planet with a glowing crystalline atmosphere.

I passed out again.

Waking, I was now inside a large white castle with beautiful music and angels surrounding a throne where God sat in a fountain of radiant light. I was immersed in water and remembered someone touching my face, comforting me.

Held in arms of love, I felt the happiest I had ever felt in my life. I was not in pain anymore and my body felt light. It was beautiful here. It felt wondrous to be loved and in the heavenly light, but I didn't want to be dead.

I wanted to be with my family on earth.

Next, I was sitting on a throne enveloped in sparkling crystal light. The glowing white light seemed to be a part of my body. I was one with light that permeated every cell.

God was here and so was I. Now sitting in a semicircle with Him and several others, His face was never revealed. I heard Him speaking of humanity's sinful state. A hologram of Earth appeared and clips of the ills and suffering of life on Earth played in front of me. Scenes of war, fighting, rioting, violence, rape, poverty, starvation, homeless refugees, polluted oceans, drought, earthquakes, hurricanes, icebergs melting, forests burning, overpopulation, and an apocalypse.

As I watched, I felt like I was in the midst of a zombie movie.

Humans were in tragic chaos. They looked crazy, out of control, and attacking each other. I do not know if it was a plague or worse, but I was mesmerized, watching and learning this would be Earth's fate when the wrath of God and judgment takes place.

The people left on Earth who refused to obey God will suffer terribly, worse than any horror movie created … because this would be real.

I cried, frightened by the violence and chaos of the zombie people. They appeared rabid, distorted, and grotesque in metal pens, trying to escape, the fate of non-believers, the unrepentant. I thought of my children and Thomas, my family. I wanted them to know of this coming battle between good and evil.

I asked, "Why does this have to happen? Couldn't humanity be given a chance?"

I heard God's voice fill the air.

> *Humanity had turned away from Me and did not obey the Ten Commandments. There is still a chance that humanity could be saved from the coming wrath.*

*Humanity is immoral and arrogant and does not
care or believe about My existence.*

His words shook me. I had believed that my life did not matter
and my actions would go unnoticed.

Thinking of my own life and separation from God, I said, "I
understand sin but it is so difficult to survive on earth and we all
make mistakes. I know firsthand how forces influenced me to sin.
I asked for mercy because sometimes life presents circumstances
that you cannot control. The family you were born into influences
and shapes the person you are. I asked for a chance to share the
truth and help humanity prepare for Jesus Christ's return and
judgment. Aren't we all a spark of the divine and worth saving?"

I was told there was not much time left. All people alive during
this age were chosen, each person played a part in Earth's fate and
humanity's survival. There was still time to
earn forgiveness. Each person must choose   **My fears were gone.**
between good and evil, Jesus or Satan.

*I have a Master Plan of Salvation and I want a
loving, respectful relationship with every person.*

The wormhole opened my thoughts, bringing a new perspective.
Too many were spiritually disconnected, and some believed they
can ask forgiveness and continue to be corrupt.

All humanity was being watched, tested, and judged by the work
they do. Our world had fallen far from God with our many sins
and lack of faith and disbelief that God exists.

Those who had blessings of wealth would fare badly if they did not help others but rather continued to live in excess and entitlement.

I do not know how long I was in Heaven, but I knew this was where I was. I did not want to leave this wonderful, beautiful place where the wormhole has taken me. But I wanted to be with my kids and with Thomas. I wanted to help my loved ones and humanity.

My last memory was being held by the most loving arms. My fears were gone. I said I would do whatever I could to help. I was enlightened that my life would be used to help humanity. How this would occur, I wasn't told.

I was forewarned. I was told some people would hate me, mock me, and I would be the butt of jokes.

It was confusing. Why would I be hated when all I wanted to do was help others?

Everyone was a sinner. What I had done was far less than some and more than others. And my own sin and suffering had allowed me to understand and have compassion. It did not call for being despised. My sin was my own and I have suffered for it.

How could I spread this message for them to understand that God was love and wanted all to pass the coming trials and tribulations, a chance for humanity to save themselves?

A voice flowed through my head … a different voice.

You will be successful in carrying this message.
Have faith and know that you are loved. I will be
with you always. You will suffer, but you must go
back to earth and do My will.

I heard His words clearly as they were revealed to me.

Let them know that each soul matters, regardless of
religion, race, nation, gender, and teach them to be
forgiving and compassionate, to not judge, to love
one another. No one is beyond salvation, even the
greatest sinners.

My wrath is great and those who continue to
disobey My commandments, committing sin will
suffer terribly. The good news is that the war is won.
Jesus won the battle with Satan, by his sacrifice
opened the door of salvation, but everyone must
choose.

It seemed like such an easy choice, having been to Hell and being
brought to Heaven gave me great hope. My last few moments in
Heaven, God held me.

Since then, I had come to believe that I was received in Heaven's
waiting room. I did not remember ever seeing any relatives or
distinct faces, yet I was comforted and loved.

There was no limit to God's mercy. His heart rejoiced when a
person repented. I knew that God loved me and was happy that
I had repented my sins and could now be saved.

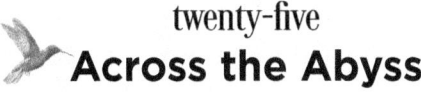

twenty-five
Across the Abyss
My heart was pounding in fear.

DAY EIGHT

Suddenly, I was standing on a narrow plank like scaffolding, about ten inches wide that spanned a vast abyss below me, and about 200 yards across to the other side. Not too far behind me was a structure that glowed eerily. It must have been the place in Hell. Looking back at the structure filled me with panic and confusion.

Where was I? Was my choice to stay here or cross the abyss?

Panic-stricken, I knew to save myself, I must walk across the abyss. My fear propelled me to move forward onto the plank. The sky was dark, and the cold wind was pushing and pulling my body, swirling as if it took turns to confuse me more.

It took an unremitting effort to move forward in the wind and not fall off the plank into the black void. I was barefoot and my feet felt frozen. The pain shot through them. It was worse than a constant stabbing of pins and needles. I knew I was unsteady, completely disoriented and in shock. But I started walking across the board, sliding my feet forward just a few inches at a time. It was all I could manage.

Keeping my eyes forward and slightly down, my heart was pounding in fear as I focused on staying upright, almost tipping

Please, please help me.

backward and falling off the plank several times. Praying repeatedly, "Please, God, please help me. Let me make it to the other side."

I knew if I fell, I would fall forever. The enormity of the abyss and blackness below me was overwhelming to my senses in me that was working.

How could this be happening so quickly?

One moment, I was filled with love and happiness... and the next moment I found myself here, alone, vulnerable, more frightened than ever.

Is the light and love of Heaven so far away that this could now be happening?

My body was trembling. It felt like an eternity, inching slowly closer to the other side. Finally, I made it across the abyss. I threw myself forward, collapsing on the ground. Oh, my God, I made it!

The woods looked and felt creepy ... beyond scary.

I lay on the ground for a few minutes, panting and dragging myself away from the edge. Looking back at where I had just come from, the board looked even narrower and seemed to sway in the wind. I was amazed I had made it safely across.

I did not know how long I had been gone. I wasn't bleeding anymore, so it had to be at least three days since I left Hazel ... since

I was taken. All I wanted was to put distance between myself and the abyss. I was still lost. I had no idea where I was.

Will I be found?

Directly ahead of me was the dark spooky forest. Crawling on hands and knees, I scurried as quickly as possible into the woods. I felt like I was being watched and wanted to hide from whatever was after me. The woods looked and felt creepy … beyond scary. I did not want to go into the dark foliage but had no choice. I was afraid something was going to grab me and drag me back to the pit or throw me into the abyss.

Making my way over the uneven forest floor, I crawled over fallen trees, around large rocks, through thick bushes covered in thorns. Their sharp points pierced and tore my exposed flesh. It felt like an enchanted forest had come alive but gone bad, attacking me from every direction.

In front of me was a large pond of mud. It looked dangerous, like quicksand that could suck me in and drown me in its depth. I wondered why this pit was here. Could it have been from the snow and rain?

My feet were on fire from the cold. I must have frostbite. Every rock or tree branch I crawled on ignited the pain within. I was forced to crawl on the ground around the perimeter of the bog, unable to stand and walk.

Staying to the right of the mud pit, I eventually came upon a dirt road. Feeling hopeful, in a moment of elation, I thought I just might find help. I didn't think I was meant to die yet; I had a message to deliver.

I pulled myself up a small hill and came upon another smaller pool of mud directly in front of me on the road. It was hard to see in the dark night and I almost plunged headfirst into the deep mud. Heart pounding, I skirted the perimeter of the second mud pit and stopped to rest under a tree. Forcing myself to a sitting position, I propped my back against the tree for added protection. I pulled my knees up to find whatever warmth they had to share.

My night was horrible. It was fraught with anxiety, fear of the dark woods, and my ordeal in hell had me terror-stricken. I was in shock at all I had seen and learned. It was extreme to go from Heaven's light and safety only to be thrown back into this dark and cold nightmare.

I desperately wanted to be with my children. They needed me, now more than ever. Their faces were so clear in my mind and dear to my heart. My throat constricted with grief. My absence was surely causing them fear and sadness. I wanted to be there for them, to be present in their lives, to provide them with love and support, and save them from the coming wrath that I saw.

They were so young and innocent and I thought about Kristiana, just a small child and my large family, how I wanted them to be okay.

I knew Thomas would be all right; he was a survivor. His life had not been easy, but he was street-smart, capable, and wise. I was blessed to know him and know his love. How I wished he was here to help and protect me, and take me home, far away from this misery, from the Hell I've been tossed into. Just thinking of Thomas, my heart ached. I loved him so much.

Would I ever see him again?

As I sat under the tree in the dark woods, I listened to the rustling movements of wildlife I could not see. I was surrounded by unseen creatures; their noises were close by as I sat motionless, frozen in fear. Now, more than ever, I was afraid for my safety. I was told there were two sides to this battle, and I had to be careful. My mind raced with thoughts I would be captured again and those hands that reach out like a lizard's tongue would grab me. I could sense a presence around me that felt menacing. I was defenseless to whatever evil lurked in the dark.

God had said I would survive, and I clung to my memory of his love and promise. But his ominous words that I would suffer greatly filled me with dread of what was to come.

How much more of this could I take? How was I going to suffer?

God said he had always been there watching me and my life and had worried about me. Lyrics from the Charlie Rich song "Behind Closed Doors" wove through my head. I thought of how few really know what goes on around most of us. How no one ever knew the abuse that went on in our house.

I reflected on a mysterious and frightening event. When I was only five years old, I was taken to a secret place where everyone was dressed in red flowing robes. I was laying on a large table and tied down. Candles were burning around me and I was surrounded by people I didn't know. They were gathered around the table chanting, and a woman who led the ritual cut me on my right hand.

I don't remember anything that happened afterward. When I woke up in my bed, I thought I had had a nightmare and saw that my right thumb was cut in the shape of the letter S, almost an inch-long cut.

Was I marked in some way as a kid?

It seemed that was when the abuse and demonic forces took hold of our home and family. I remembered running from my stepdad and hiding in a closet so he would not find me. Jayne came into the closet with me and tried to protect me from my stepdad who was trying to pull me out of the closet, kicking me in the face and head with his steel-toed boots.

Someone had let the dog out of the yard, and he blamed me. I was frightened of his anger. My face and head had been battered and bloodied. Jayne had tried to protect me and taken the brunt of his attack. I felt deep sadness that I had been unwanted and hated by my stepdad.

I leaned my head against my knees and tried to reconcile the violence of my childhood with my new knowledge that God had been there. At the time I thought God did not care or love me to allow this to happen. I now knew that his heart grieved for us.

Other than my abusive stepdad, I never had a father, and it was an absence sorely missed. My only father figure had been my grandfather who I rarely saw once I started school. I had been embittered at life's injustice. My new awareness changed my perspective of my earlier life experiences. Now I was free to let go of the past and forgive, knowing I had a Father in Heaven who loved and watched over me, every day.

It was comforting to know one day God would bring me back to Heaven, and all that had transpired was meant to be.

With new insight, I had closure on my divorce and some of the guilt and sadness I was carrying, and I could let it go. I was relieved to know that the divorce was not the fault of either one of us. It was meant to happen.

Our lives had been turned upside down and everything had changed. We were loving parents. We had been a happy family, living the American dream … a dream that changed so suddenly.

twenty-six

The Shaman's Call

Leaning against the tree,
I finally slept sitting upright.

It was common that shamans had ancestors that were sometimes referred to as Curanderas, and the healing ability was passed on to another generation. Before the separation and divorce, I loved and believed in Jesus Christ. I often prayed for us … that God's spirit would bless us both to become Godlier, in a spiritual sense. I was not prepared for the spiritual journey and turmoil that would change our lives forever.

The signs of a shaman awakening included seeing your spiritual animal. My spiritual animal was the hummingbird. I also have several other totems, along with the bat. I remembered a camping trip where a bat flew directly at my head and landed in my hair. Bat is symbolic of shamanic rebirth. I had been rebirthed, given a second chance.

The signs of a shaman awakening included developing a love for nature. That shift happened when I began hiking, experiencing the freshness and beauty of the mountains, and embracing what nature brings with its kaleidoscope of seasons and colors.

The awakening included connecting strongly with animals and appreciating that their presence can bring a message to you in your life. Sometimes a near death experience occurs, something that I felt multiple times over several days.

It was often with great struggle that shamans broke free from their illness and awakened to the truth. By learning how to cure themselves, they also learned how to heal others. Was it connected to becoming a Reiki master? Or was there more to it?

Was this to be my path?

My shaman transformation resulted in an almost complete traumatic separation from my life. Because of the difficult initiation process, shamans are often called wounded healers: finding it hard to fit in with others; considered eccentric, or different, weird. Indeed, I had been wounded.

It can be described as *walking between two worlds:* the earthly plane and heavenly plane. Or it could also be the place we call Hell. I have walked through Hell.

I remembered a very vivid dream where I was able to astral travel, where my body stayed put, but my spirit takes a journey. I was sitting in a stadium in outer space surrounded by every alien lifeform imaginable. It was as if I was in the middle of a *Star Wars* movie. At the podium, the speaker

I felt my body drained by the intense fear and stress.

was talking about Earth's many human troubles: the fighting amongst humanity; concern for war; and man's capability to destroy earth.

Humanity needed an intervention—if Earth was destroyed, the effects would reverberate throughout the solar system in a negative way. Who would step forward and help them? Watching myself in the dream, I stepped up to the podium and offered to go and help.

It was ironic that now I was being called to deliver a message of hope to humanity. I had no idea how this was to come about.

Leaning against the tree, I finally slept sitting upright. I felt my body drained by the intense fear and stress of my journey across the plank and through the dark woods. My mind was tired. I was exhausted.

twenty-seven

The Magical Forest

*Sharp needles of pain were shooting
through the soles of my feet and up my legs.*

DAY NINE

In the morning light, I could see about a hundred yards ahead
a clearing in the forest. There stood a small wooden cabin with a
wood deck and two lawn loungers! I could not believe my eyes!
At first, I doubted it was there; thinking of the first house that
magically disappeared: the illusion.

I stood up slowly. I was so excited. With the first small step I took,
I winced at the pain in my feet. The cabin in front of me became
the ultimate super magnet. My eyes continued to stare at it with
each step. If I took my eyes off of it, I feared it would disappear.
My hope soared.

Was I going to be rescued? What if no one was home?

My focus so intent on the house, I vaguely remember making my
way through the trees into the clearing. When I finally stepped on
the deck, I knew it was real!

"Oh, thank you, God!" I yelled out loud, so relieved to find help.
The stress quickly drained from my tense body, and now I wanted
to just lie down on the lounger and get off the cold ground.

Looking around, it did not appear anyone was in the vicinity. I heard no sound that would tell me a person was close by. A sense of foreboding came over me as I sat resting on the edge of the lounger. The clearing allowed sunlight in. My feet were an unsightly mess. They were swollen at least three times the size of my normal foot. The bottoms were black, as if I had walked through ashes—bleeding, dirty, and with all the lacerations ... looking like raw hamburger. Cuts covered my legs from my feet to my thighs.

My blue gym shorts were stiff with dried blood that had flowed freely a few days ago. I was a complete mess: my legs crusted in scabs; my hair was grungy and tangled.

Hobbling around to the front door, I knocked and knocked, calling out, "Hello, hello." The square pane of glass on the door had a small curtain blocking any view inside. I tried the doorknob; it was locked. I briefly considered breaking into the cabin to find a phone, but I didn't want to invade someone's property or commit a crime. My unsteady stagger brought me around the left side of the cabin. I peeked into a window.

The fear came rushing back as I looked inside. I could see the room glowed with light from several rows of twenty, or more, televisions and computers. Every TV and computer was on, and the screens were constantly changing channels. It reminded me of a scene out of a Robin Cook novel, and I was horrified. I remembered the big screen and my movie that had played before I was pulled up by God.

My senses reeled; this place felt unsafe. This place was bad. My intuition told me I needed to get away from here fast. I had a sense that whoever lived here had a connection to the side I needed to fear. I turned away from the cabin and saw an old red pickup truck parked way off to the side. Thinking maybe the truck had keys inside it, I slowly made my way to the truck.

Walking west on the rocky road was excruciatingly painful as the rocks dug into my torn flesh. I thought of my favorite ice cream as a kid, Rocky Road, with each painful step I took and could not help but wonder at life's twists and coincidence.

The red paint of the truck was dulled by time. I'd guess it to be 50 to 60 years old.

I felt like I should not be here.

Opening the driver's door, a cloud of old dusty air escaped. The floorboards were littered with trash, old Coca-Cola bottles, and tools. I wondered how long this stuff had been here.

The bench seat was covered with a layer of thick dust. I slid across the seat to check the ignition … no keys. But I found two rings with a bunch of keys on each in the glove compartment.

My hope soared. The ignition key *must* be one of the dozen or so keys. I tried each one. None of them worked. I felt like I should not be here. This was private property and I was trespassing, but I was desperate.

Being inside the truck was eerie. The air felt suffocating and I felt trapped. Everything was so old … and so odd. The open door had shut on its own when I first slid across the seat. As much as I wanted to lie down and rest, I could not do that … not here.

This place felt evil.

Hurriedly, I put the keys back with the registration papers in the glove compartment and exited the truck. I took deep, cleansing breaths, thankful to be in the fresh air.

Feeling a sense of doom, I knew I had to leave here. I looked around, trying to decide which way I should go. I could hear the sound of traffic echoing through the field but unable to see anything beyond a large hill in the distance. I decided I should follow the road but stay to the side where I wouldn't be seen.

When I was in Heaven, I was told there is a division, two sides that are battling against each other, one side was Jesus and the Holy Trinity, the other side was Satan and all who followed him. This battle was for souls. Humanity was mostly oblivious to what was happening, as I once was. I needed to be careful who I trusted.

I couldn't walk anymore.

I was terrified that whoever belonged to the cabin and truck would come for me. I had seen what Hell looked like and never wanted to be near it again. This place felt evil. I had to escape.

I couldn't walk anymore. I sat on the ground and scooted myself across the rocky field of wild sage and small shrubbery on my butt. The sun felt wonderful on my cold body, and I breathed in the aromatic sage. As I pulled myself along the ground, my back felt like it was on fire. Remembering the brutal beating I had received, my back throbbed with pain. My thin woolen jacket was scratchy and abrasive on my raw, wounded back. The fibers were sticking to my oozing wounds. I wished I had not burned my shirt and bra.

Remembering the cabin, my gut told me I needed to get away from here as fast as I could. My thirst was immense. I had picked up another pebble for my mouth. The saliva it created helped.

I prayed for help. *God, I need your help. I'm lost, thirsty and I don't know which way to go. Please send me a sign to direct me.* Right then a beautiful hummingbird appeared, flying circles around me. I was entranced and delighted. Its colorful little body zoomed back and forth, spiraling and circling above my head. It kept coming back when I didn't follow it.

I followed the hummingbird and headed north again. I would do what I did before when I looked for signs of two and connect to the energy and living earth around me. I felt blessed to see my totem, my spirit animal, and to be given this guidance. God had answered my prayers.

I felt brief happiness, optimistic that I would somehow get myself out of my predicament. This seemed like an omen, a sign that I would be okay. I wasn't so alone. God was helping me.

Then the hummingbird flew away, and I was unsure of what direction to go. I kept hoping it would come back. It didn't. As I was debating what to do, a huge bumblebee came buzzing around me.

It circled around my body, buzzing loudly and flew north, as the hummingbird had. I had never seen a bumblebee so large. Its body was at least two inches long, all furry, yellow, and black. It was a delight to see. Despite my situation, I was loving this time with nature and all its beauty.

As I scooted forward, I recalled playing outside in the creek as a child. We kids built dams in the gutters, made mudpies, and caught crawdads. Thoughts of riding my stingray bike with the banana seat on dirt hills put a smile on my wounded face. The pebble was creating limited saliva. I desperately needed water. My mind envisioned a glass of ice-cold lemonade; how wonderful that would taste. I had not had water since I left Hazel. My thirst was greater than my hunger at that moment. I desperately wanted to be clean; to wash away the dirt and blood and soothe my aching body.

I knew it was useless to daydream about food, but there had to be water somewhere. I just needed to find it and again I prayed for guidance. Picking up another small stone and brushing it off, I placed it on my tongue. I felt my mouth hydrate.

The bumblebee now became my guide. I continued north, scooting on my butt, making my way down a steep ravine, lifting my body over rocks and around shrubs. As I prayed for help, a colorful butterfly appeared. Confident that God was speaking to me through these lovely creatures, I continued to scoot down the mountain following the butterfly. I had crossed the road 200-300 feet back and was sitting on the ground in full sun and it was getting hot. My jacket was itchy and trapping hot air on my body.

I was beginning to doubt myself. Should I have stayed on the road? I looked down and saw a brown spider about the size of my thumbnail. I asked the little spider to guide me to water and watched as it seemed to do a little dance and crawl north. Again, I followed my new friend, the spider. At one time in my life, I was terrified of spiders. A relative used to catch them and pin me down, holding a spider's body inches from my face, as I cried and screamed to get loose.

Over the years I would squish any spider I saw in the house. My values changed in the last few years where I now appreciated all God's creatures. Instead of killing a spider, I now captured it and released it outside. Finding the little creature fascinating with its dance, I scooted after it. At times, it seemed to stop, waiting for me to catch up as it led the way.

The landscape was changing. There were bigger shrubs and trees. It was difficult to scoot over the ground, so I crawled on my knees and climbed over the rocks, pinecones, and dead tree limbs. I loved the fresh, fragrant smell of pine needles and enjoyed the beauty of the rugged mountain.

Layers upon layers of pine needles created a spongy, soft ground that I could crawl over. I had made it down **I felt instant relief.** a steep rocky ravine and could see a small creek at the bottom. Energized, I hurriedly pulled myself along to get to the water.

Sliding forward on my belly, I made it to the creek. Cupping the cold running water in my hands, I splashed my face. It felt amazing. I drank handfuls of ice-cold water, finally feeling my belly full. Nothing had ever tasted so refreshing and sweet.

Sitting up, I put my burning feet in the water. I felt instant relief. I vowed that I would not leave my water source again. I decided this was where I would spend the night, close to the creek. It had taken me a full day to get here. Resting under a tree I dozed off, waking when it was dusk.

I looked around for shelter—a place to sleep for the night—and crawled up the creekbank to discover a large hollowed-out tree stump. It was large enough that I could crawl inside and have shelter from the cold. I desperately wanted to be warm. The frigid air was settling in, and my exposed flesh was so cold. I tried not to think of the insects, spiders, and whatever else that might live inside the stump. Sharp needles of aching, intense pain were shooting through the soles of my feet and up my legs.

The stump was about three feet high. I was just able to lift my leg over and heave myself up into it. As night fell, I constantly turned myself to the left and then the right, trying to generate warmth. It was mind-numbing cold. It was all I could think about … that and my hunger.

It had been at least a week since I last ate anything. I longed for a burger and fries, or pizza. All my favorite foods filled my mind. Trying to put thoughts of food out of my mind, I planned for tomorrow. I remember Thomas telling me that eventually a water source, or river, would run into a town. So that is what I would do. Follow the small creek and see where it leads … tomorrow.

I fell asleep thinking about my children and Thomas, missing them so much. I wondered how they were getting along without me there.

Were they okay? Will I see them again?

I was trying to remain optimistic. And I was grateful that at least I had water close by and some protection from the cold air.

twenty-eight

Severe Frostbite

*I wondered if I had made the right decision
in not staying on the road.*

Little sleep came that night. Pain, exhaustion, and my aching body had kept me awake most of it. After a few brief hours of sleep, I woke with the sun and climbed out of the stump. A jolt of pain coursed through my body as my back scraped against the wood. I felt frozen; it hurt to move anything. In great pain, I fell onto the ground. Looking at my feet, they were not recognizable: swollen, cut up, and black, like they had been in a fire. I turned my head away. It was too distressing to look at them. Even if I was found, my feet would never be the same again.

Would I even have them?

Crawling back to the stream, I plunged my frozen burning feet into the water. The coldness numbed the pain. At the same time, I scooped up water and drank handful after handful. I gazed into the watery depth of the stream that flowed and wondered at the little gold flakes sparkling in the sunrays that lit the water.

Then I wondered if the water was safe to drink. *Was it?* It would not have mattered … I would have drunk whatever I could find at this point. It looked okay—clear and pure. I knew that this water was from the mountain snowmelt, not dirtied by humans.

I needed warmth to defrost from my exposure to the cold night. The small creek was nestled in a ravine that was shadowed by the mountain. I followed the creek that was going west, downhill, scooting slowly and painfully. It felt like a long and never-ending journey over the forest floor. I felt safer here, hidden, and away from the cabin and road … and the red truck, but the air was colder. My consolation was the warm rays of sunshine that began to illuminate the early morning.

Moving about 20 feet away from the creek, I stopped. I had to pee. It seemed like I hadn't peed for days. Now, it was an easier task as I sat on the ground. As I scooted away from the small puddle I created, the dark yellow of the urine was a reminder of how dehydrated my body was.

I wondered if I had made the right decision in not staying on the road. Maybe someone would have come along, but I couldn't risk falling into the evil I had witnessed. My promise to myself was to stay close to the water. It was the only thing that could keep me alive now.

Above were clear blue skies and my body warmed to the sun's rays, as if a special bath of them had been created just for me. My body embraced the warmth that it finally felt. As I laid on the ground warming up, my feet started burning yet again.

I needed to mentally work on healing myself. I needed time to meditate and do the Reiki I knew on my body. But I couldn't. The exhaustion that had trapped my body, left me with a feeling of paralysis from creating the exertion I needed. I had no energy to channel anything. All I could do was lie there and rest. What minimal energy I had was spent in getting away from the abyss and the cabin. My safety had been my priority; self-healing had to wait.

Scooting back to the stream, I put my feet into the ice-cold water again. It seemed contrary to get them wet and cold again, but the pain was so intense I was willing to do anything for relief. Immediately, the pain subsided. My feet looked horrible. The creekwater had cleaned some of the dirt away and what I saw now was black flesh, blistered and rotting away.

My stomach now groaned, begging for food.

I remembered times of hunger when I lived my childhood in poverty. I was thin and undernourished.

As a junior in high school, I lived in my own apartment, went to school, and worked two part-time jobs. I drove an old beater car that used to make popping noises from a bad catalytic converter whenever I drove it.

Paying my own rent and expenses at the age of 17 left me very little money to buy food. Often, I had to choose between buying gas for my car and groceries. Somehow, I managed, but my diet was mostly canned soup. A big treat was a McDonald's cheese-burger and fries. How I wished I had that cheeseburger and fries right now.

My imagination took over—playing out a future with no feet. I was certain they would be amputated, and I would have to make the best of the situation. What would it be like to lose my feet? My life would be so different confined to a wheelchair. All I could envision were stumps at the end of my legs.

I knew two things: my body was exhausted, and it was starving. I had so many vivid memories of food. I sat thinking about my past, when I had been hungry at other times in my life. It did not compare to this empty famished feeling of my body right now.

I used to enjoy cooking tasty meals for my family. In my mind, food became an obsession. I was daydreaming of a slice of pizza loaded with sausage, mushrooms, black olives, generous sauce, and mozzarella cheese, sprinkled with parmesan, red pepper, and crust to dip in honey, or a cheddar cheeseburger on a wheat bun, onion slices, pickles, mustard, and salty crisp fries with ketchup. My mouth salivated, thinking of how delicious each mouthful would be.

The pines of the forest reminded me of Thanksgiving time and I saw a plate piled high with turkey, another favorite. Mom's pecan stuffing, mashed potatoes covered in turkey gravy, sweet potato casserole topped with toasted marshmallows, and Grandma's homemade dinner rolls.

My stomach now groaned, begging for food. I fed my mind a heaping plate of spaghetti with sausage and peppers and a buttery slice of garlic bread, plus a beef and bean burrito smothered in homemade green chili with tender pork, melted cheese, lettuce and tomatoes.

It was agony to remember so clearly eating delicious food. I could almost taste and smell it as my stomach cramped in emptiness. I could feel my body shrinking, my legs looked thinner, and I felt lighter. I felt so empty.

Finding a sunny spot, I fell into a deep sleep on the ground. Waking up to my feet burning in pain, I again dipped into the creek for relief. I needed to be moving to find help, but it was already turning dusk, and my body was barely able to move.

twenty-nine
My Log Coffin

As each day passed, my family felt further away.
I feared I would never see them again.

EVENING OF THE NINTH DAY

Dragging myself slowly across the forest floor, I was looking for any kind of shelter and warmth from the bitter cold. I spotted a fallen trunk some twenty feet ahead. Fortunately, it was another hollowed-out log. This time it looked big enough for me to lay down inside—maybe ten feet long. I needed to sleep.

Kelly ... you have to keep moving ... you can't give up.

With sheer will, I crawled and dragged myself on my hands and knees, forcing my badly bruised and injured body to make it to the log.

Inside the log were several inches of pine needles, leaves, wood chips, and other debris ... and most likely, a lot of bugs. With one arm, I swept what I could out. Silently, I said I was sorry, a moment of remorse for any little critters I was displacing.

Pulling my body up into the log was a difficult ordeal. The narrow walls of the log were scraping my back, now throbbing in pain, unable to lay on it. I stayed on my side as dusk quickly faded into dark.

The frosty air from the stream created a cold that penetrated to my bones. With the heavy pine coverage, no light was illuminated from the stars above. It was the blackest of night. I put my hand a few inches in front of my face and was unable to see it.

The total darkness filled me with immobilizing fear of what the night might bring. Unable to move around, it felt like a coffin … so claustrophobic. I listened to the sounds of the forest, the rustling noises of creatures moving around me and what had become the eerie sense I was being watched. At times, it felt like spiders were crawling over my body, but I was helpless to brush them off or move away.

Total aloneness left me with only my thoughts. Again, my childhood, my upbringing, and what I had experienced since I abandoned Hazel left me to think about what I had suffered, learned, and been spared from. How I wished I would have known about man's fall, angels, demons, and sin. I would have been wiser in the choices I had made.

If I had known what my life experiences were to be, I think I would have acted and chosen differently. I felt frozen and my thoughts told me that God was mysterious.

Despite the remorse I felt watching my life movie, I knew I was not a terrible person. Life had been challenging at times, to say the least, and I did what I could to survive on my own. My sins were really a very small part of my life, but they were haunting. I felt like God had forgiven me but I was called to reflect on my past and pray for anyone I had harmed or had harmed me.

Feeling overwhelmed by the whole chain of events, I tried to remember all that I was told. During my time in Heaven, I learned that all of my actions throughout my whole life were known. My life experiences were meant to happen, including sin and suffering. Nothing was a coincidence. Many times, in my past, I wondered why my life was so difficult. Just when I had consistency and a plan, something drastic would happen and my plans would get messed up.

I had no idea where I was.

Now I knew differently. My life struggles were meant for me to experience and learn, to develop compassion and empathy for others. I knew how it felt to be compelled to do something I did not really want to do.

This I now know ... yes, demon spirits are real and here on earth. All the world religions I have read about mentioned a dark force at battle with good. Countless times in the Bible, Jesus talks about casting out demons and demon possession, and spirits that roam the earth searching for vulnerable people to inhabit and compel them to sin. In the evenings, wherever He was, villagers would bring those they believed were possessed by demons to Him to drive out the spirits and cure them from illnesses with His words.

I thought awareness of this supernatural happening was half the battle won, understanding that certain sinful behaviors might allow an open entry for one to become possessed. I used to think possession was something obvious, like in the movie *The Exorcist*. But it could be subtle and hidden. Jesus knew the battle we would face and with compassion and mercy

It felt like spiders were crawling over my body.

offers forgiveness for all humanity. By His sacrifice and death on the cross, He won the battle with Satan.

It was shocking to learn that nothing was hidden from God. Every single moment in our lives was known and recorded, all to be used for the day we will be judged and sent to Heaven, Hell, or Purgatory. He knew everything about me when I was there with Him.

There have been people in my life who have caused me sorrow. I thought I could never forgive or forget what they had done. But I learned forgiving others allows me to be forgiven for my own sins. Justice was not for me to seek, as all stand before Jesus to be judged by our actions.

I was miserable lying in the hollow log. Unable to move around, it felt like a coffin, confining and boxed in. I was forced to lay on my left side the whole night, peering into complete darkness, alert to every sound around me.

I spent most of this night unable to sleep, terrified of the dark and my memories of Hell, powerless to escape my nightmarish torments.

As each day passed, my family felt further away. I feared I would never see them again. I prayed to God that I would be with them again and I heard His voice.

You will be okay and survive.

I had no idea where I was. All the things that I had done wrong that led up to where I was and what I was experiencing took over my thoughts. I knew that I had made a serious mistake by my failure not to tell anyone where I was going. But there were other failures, too:

- not having my phone;

- not having a flashlight;

- not taking the space blanket with me;

- not having better shoes; and

- not having extra water in the car.

There was so many things that I should have had when Hazel got stuck.

The regret for the fear and pain my family was experiencing because of my actions was deep. Not a day had passed since I left Denver where I was not sorry for putting them through this and wanted to be with them so badly.

If only I had another chance …

If only I survive this ordeal …

I would appreciate my loved ones and love them unconditionally.

I made it through another freezing cold, fitful night with only bits of sleep. The welts on my back throbbed in pain, a constant reminder of my beating and punishment in Hell.

I could not wait for sunrise so I could see again … and then, so I could drag my ice-cold body to thaw out in the sunshine.

thirty
The River

My legs and feet were being stabbed repeatedly with sizzling hot probes.

DAY TEN

As soon as the sun lit up the sky, I inched out of the log, desperate to get warm and regretting my choice of sleeping in the log. My body was stiff with cold, adding to the severe pain I was experiencing in my frozen feet. *This must be what it feels like to be hit by a train.* Any movement I attempted was done in an extremely slow motion.

Even though it was June, here at the bottom of the ravine, the air was frigid—frigid as winter time in the Rocky Mountains. My frosty breath created little clouds of icy vapors as I struggled to crawl up the ravine on my hands and knees to seek warmth.

It seemed like forever to get to the top of the creekbank. Seeing a large boulder, I made my way to it and climbed on top, ignoring the pine needles and a variety of insects—many dead, some alive. As starved as I was, eating bugs hadn't been an option for me. I had no concept of time but the sun was still low. Exhausted from crawling, I curled in a ball on the cold rock, waiting for the sun to warm it … and me.

 As it rose, I looked up at a cloudless, brilliant blue sky. I had a new appreciation for sunshine. It felt so amazing to be warmed on the rock. I was so grateful to be out of the log, able to move and stretch my body. I felt alive in a sense, a part of the forest, as my body adapted to the rays landing on it. As the sun continued to rise, my feet began to defrost. The piercing, burning pain created felt like my legs and feet were being stabbed repeatedly with sizzling hot probes.

Scooting on my butt off the boulder and back down the ravine, I made my way back to the stream. **I was a filthy, bloody mess.** In my feet went, cooling the extreme burning I was feeling. Drinking handfuls of water, I filled my stomach, easing the hunger pangs that twisted my gut.

Now, being filled with water, my curiosity took over. *Where does this stream go?* Lifting myself to my awkward crawl, I followed it downhill. The stream flowed into a river.

In the warm sun, I took off my clothes and plunged forward into the waist-deep freezing cold water. Breathing fast from the shock of the cold, I quickly dunked my entire body, my hair flowing around me. I shook it out, rubbing my scalp and hair. Once more I went underwater, running my hands over my body scrubbing as if I had soap.

Crawling out of the water, I lay by the river's edge, feeling energized and so happy to be clean. Grabbing my shorts and underwear, I scrubbed them, glad to finally wash out the dirt and blood. After wringing them out, I looked around taking in my surroundings.

The river looked to be about 50 feet wide. The spring melt-off was fast with white-caps, waves that peaked, crashing over and forming again.

I needed to dry off and dry my wet clothes. Spotting a large rock, I crawled over with clothes in hand and pulled myself on top. Placing them on the rock, I sat up, running my fingers through my long tangled hair.

I realized it was very possible that I could lose my toes ... or even my feet.

It felt amazing to be clean again and warmed by the sun, but it had taken its toll. I had so little energy left. I needed rest ...sleep.

Wishing I had a comb, I twisted my hair into a French braid, looking around for something to tie it. I fleetingly thought I could use bark from a tree, but I was too tired to get off the rock. It was a long process to smooth out my hair because it was so thick and wavy. I was overdue for a haircut. My hair hung down to the middle of my back. Now, it was just in the way, wild around my face and annoying.

Staring at my feet, I realized it was very possible that I could lose toes ... or even my feet, maybe even part of my legs. The black flesh was starting to discolor my ankles and calves. I decided that if that should happen, I would make the best of the circumstance and be grateful to survive. But I needed to find help soon, or I would lose my life.

On the other side of the river was a steep embankment that I knew I could climb if I could get to the other side. I just needed to rest. I was sure a road was close by.

Naked, I lay back on the rock and slept deeply.

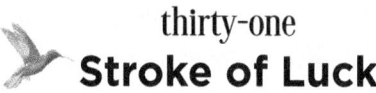

thirty-one
Stroke of Luck

*Feeling my life force growing weaker,
I wondered if my body heat would
keep me alive to see another day.*

I woke up when I heard voices nearby. People talking and laughing. I quickly put on my underwear, shorts, and jacket and desperately yelled, over and over: "Help, hello?" They did not hear me, and their voices became fainter.

They were gone. I gave up yelling. My voice was hoarse. I crawled back to the river to cool my defrosting feet.

I sat watching the waves crashing in the water and wondered … could I swim across the river? Did I have the strength?

I remember a time when I was tubing a mountain river. I fell off the inner tube and almost drowned. I couldn't get my footing and the current was pushing me downstream toward the chutes, a narrow waterfall with large boulders.

Luckily, a nearby fisherman saw me in distress and quickly reached out to me with his fishing pole to grab.

Now, there was no fisherman to help me. This water was deep and shockingly cold. It felt much colder than the stream. I would probably drown or die from hypothermia if I attempted to swim. Then I thought that if I had a raft, I might be able to make it downstream and find people … cabins … and help.

I set about gathering branches, dragging them to the side of the river. Weaving strips of bark that I pulled off from the branches around the dead wood and tying the branches with knots to hold them together. It was nice to be busy, doing something that might help me.

When I finished with the small raft, it was about 2 ½ feet wide and 3 ½ feet long. I pushed it into the water and tried to climb on it. I had another large stick to push off with and use as a buffer against rocks.

In just a few minutes of sitting on the raft it fell apart, the sticks floating away in the current. I guess that was a stroke of luck that it fell apart when I was still next to the river's edge. If I had been any further along, I'd have been in the middle of the rapids and surely drowned.

Disappointed my plan did not work, I felt disheartened. My hopes were crushed like the raft. Once again, I crawled back to the rock, pulling my body on top wondering if, and how, I would get rescued. I was completely drained of energy, weak, and weary to the bone. It was unlikely someone would find me on this rock, yet I knew I did not have the energy to crawl much farther.

This time, not bothering to sweep away insects, I collapsed. I desperately needed to rest. So far, I had not been bit or stung by anything, although I would not really be able to distinguish if I had, with all the cuts and abrasions that covered my body. Thankfully, it must have been too early in the season for mosquitoes to be out, my nemesis in the past. Unless I was covered in bug spray, they attacked me relentlessly, leaving dime- and nickel-sized red welts on my body that itched for days.

Soaking up the last of the sun's rays on the rock, I could feel
the chill of night and the rock turning cold beneath me. I feared
another freezing night on the mountain. As much as I loved the
beauty of the forest, it was terrifying to be alone in the woods in
the pitch blackness for another night, exposed and vulnerable.

I did not know how much longer I could continue to survive
without food. My body was starving, and I could not think of any
food source other than digging for insects. The mere thought of it
was disgusting, and I knew it wasn't something I was going to do.

As each day passed, I knew that I was weaker. I felt my life force
had grown weaker. My family—their faces—were now blurring,
standing in a distant tunnel. I could no longer see them clearly in
my mind. Could my body heat keep me
alive to see another day?

**The rock became
bone-chilling cold,
like a giant ice cube.**

Forcing myself to get off the rock, I
dragged myself to the ground. I crawled around gathering fallen
pine tree boughs and built a small shelter, stacking the branches
against each other like a teepee. It was just large enough that I
could crawl inside, and I hoped it would retain some warmth.

For a moment I considered sleeping on a large rock to be off the
ground, but as soon as the sun set, the rock became bone-chilling
cold, like a giant ice cube. Remembering my previous night of
misery in the open log, I decided I would rather sleep on the
ground and hope the branches would keep me hidden from
whatever was tailing me. I still sensed its presence—whatever
"it" was.

Sitting inside my makeshift shelter, I prayed and tried to channel energy. Holding my foot in my hands, it felt frozen; the coldness felt impenetrable. Closing my eyes, I imagined I was back in Heaven, in the light, and that I was rooted in earth. Asking for God's help to save my feet, I meditated for several hours, working to bring life back into each foot.

I had always been squeamish about tending to injuries, especially my own. The sight of my mangled feet made it difficult to look at them and especially touch them, but I knew it was necessary and would help with what little energy I had in me.

It was difficult to focus on healing. I was shell-shocked and worn-out from stress. Eventually, I felt the energy coursing through my hands. I felt a tingling in my feet. Hopefulness came into my hands.

As I sat in my little teepee doing Reiki, I could hear the thrashing sound of a large animal moving around. The snapping and breaking of tree branches sounded very close by. I knew I had not put enough thought into choosing a place to sleep, but it had taken all my energy to gather the boughs and I was exhausted.

I was in a small circular clearing with large rocks and boulders on one side and trees all around. I was not hidden at all, just right out in the middle where I could easily be grabbed. I expected at any moment I would be attacked and waited in dread for my coming death. I was certain "it" could sense my fear. Eventually the noises stopped, and the creature moved away. Whatever animal it was had left me alone. Afraid it would come back, I faced another long night in constant fear.

Lying on my side, I curled into a ball trying to create warmth, and worried about my family. I prayed that Paige and Ryan were being supported by family and tried to reassure myself that they were strong, smart, resilient and would be able to overcome my absence in their lives.

Facing my own mortality, all I could think of was my family. I realized how much they meant to me, their presence and love in my life had been a precious gift and memory that I now clung to. My heart ached to be with them again.

I thought about Paige, my sweet angel. Words could not even express how much I cared for her. Sad tears rolled down my cheeks … how I missed her. Memories filled my mind of our life together: her birth; the joy of being her mom; watching her grow up; her kind and gentle personality. She was loving and kind in a world that could be cruel. Paige was so young and innocent and I wanted to be there for her, to shelter and protect her from harm. I could see her beautiful smile lighting up her eyes, hear her voice calling me momma.

And I felt her sorrow and knew she felt afraid for me … and to be alone. I imagined that she could hear my thoughts. The love that we shared was powerful and unending. "My sweet Paige, I'm still here. I'll never leave you," I whispered out loud. I prayed that God would keep her safe, surround her with loving angels and let me live to see her again.

I breathed a ragged breath, tears welling in my eyes thinking of Ryan, my beloved son. I cried for my boy that had recently become a young man. My heart ached when I remembered his face, dear to me. From the moment I held him and throughout the years, he filled my heart with love. Easygoing, he always had a positive nature and outlook on life, rarely expressing his feelings. But I knew him well; words were not necessary.

I reminisced about the love and life we have shared, missing him increased my tears. In his early years he wanted to be with me constantly and would cry if we were apart. Now, he was independent and busy in his life. I desperately wanted to be there for him and support him through his life journey.

We had a strong bond. I could feel his worry and sadness. And I was sure that he knew that I was still alive. I hoped he was doing okay. I said another prayer asking God to be with him and bring him love and support and bring me home so I could hold him and tell him how much I loved him again.

I prayed that Thomas was helping Paige and Ryan get through this. An empty sadness filled me when I thought about my husband.

Thomas was my best friend and I loved him. We had been together ten years and had a connection that seemed like it was our destiny to be together. Even though he was far away from me now, I could feel his presence and him willing me to hang on and be strong. I was not giving up. Tomorrow I will try to find help. I still had hope but at this moment it seemed like my death was imminent.

I thought about Bob and Boomer, our beloved pups. They brought much love to our family with their presence. I remembered how we used to snuggle in bed. They would curl up next to me, warm and happy to be petted. Most nights, just before falling asleep I would give them Reiki and would receive telepathic impressions of their thoughts.

Working on Boomer once, I learned that he was sad and hurt that he had been kicked in anger. I received mental pictures of their memories that had been traumatic to them and felt the fear they held in their bodies, like a blip on a computer, and then it would pass, sometimes with the passing of gas or jerky, twitchy movements of their bodies.

One time I had taken the dogs to Cherry Creek Reservoir and Boomer slid on an icy spot, his back legs had splayed out into splits, and he could not walk. I lifted him off the ice and did Reiki on his hips. After a short time, he was able to walk and run again. I had been grateful for the gift I had and the healing it brought.

I knew Bob and Boomer were a welcome distraction for Paige, Ryan, and Thomas. I missed sleeping on my bed and remembered how their presence was comforting. If they were with me, their bodies would keep me warm and they would protect me from forest animals.

I fell asleep wondering how my life was going to be used.

I was stunned at what had happened to me. Heaven, the beautiful light, the message, and love that I experienced—Christ's love. I was grateful to have escaped the gates of Hell and its torments.

I was joyful and amazed, in awe of what had been revealed. It was life-changing to learn that Heaven and Hell are real. It gave me hope. My faith was renewed in Christ. I prayed for myself and my family, reassured by the Voice that I would survive.

Mindful of my sore and bruised back, I tried to lay on one side, then the other, flipping over throughout the night, trying to find relief from my ever-present pain.

I fell asleep wondering how my life was going to be used to bring God's message to a world that needed God more than ever.

thirty-two
Four-Legged Angel

There was little life energy within me.
I might not wake up if I fell asleep.

DAY ELEVEN

During the night, my makeshift teepee shelter had collapsed around me. Upon waking, I saw the pine tree boughs scattered on and around me.

I sat in the early morning frost, remembering that I was still lost, feeling desolate and incapable of moving. My body was chilled to the bone, sluggish and weak. I was desperate to get warm. I knew I was losing weight. My body was changing in front of me. My flesh was cold as ice. My bones were clearly visible under the thin layer of skin that covered them.

My will to survive finally moved me to crawl to a boulder and climb on top waiting for the sun's rays to warm my body. I had made it through another night!

I had no idea how long I slept. I have no concept of time passing. Drifting off again, I woke when I could not stand the burning in my defrosting feet.

Half falling and sliding off the rock, I moved into my crawl to get back to the river. I carefully dipped my feet into the water to cool them down from the temporary defrosting that was periodically happening. On my knees, I filled my cupped hands with water and drank, but I couldn't get enough water. I drank again and again, trying to satisfy my hunger pangs with the refreshing water. In my mind, I was drinking lemonade—a mixture of sweet and tart.

I knew that my body was ebbing away. There was little life energy within me. I knew help needed to arrive right away. It was hard to stay awake and I felt so weak, unable to move. My thoughts were foggy. My family's faces became half-formed images that seemed to fade as I struggled to remember them.

All I wanted to do was lay in the sun and sleep with my feet in the river. But I couldn't do that. I had to keep moving! I might

With those thoughts, the light came closer.

not wake up if I fell asleep again.

It was a strenuous process, dragging my body along the ground, sapping the little life energy I had. Pain vibrated throughout my body. As I lay immobile near the water, I felt like I was losing consciousness. It was a receding and flowing feeling. I shut my eyes and I thought about Heaven. With those thoughts, the light came closer.

Looking up into the sky, a white shimmering cloud was above

I am dying and I need help.

me. I saw my grandmother's face in it. She was speaking to me. I heard her voice saying, "Mijita, it is not your time to go to Heaven. You have to stay here and do the work you need to do. Your daughter and your son need you."

"I'm too injured and weak to walk. I am lost, Grandma," I said in a weak voice. "I am dying and I need help now."

Her words were clear. "Don't worry, you will be safe, Mijita."

I succumbed to the sleep that was creeping up on me. *I didn't feel safe. Grandma, how am I going to be safe?* were my last thoughts before my eyes closed.

A noise suddenly awakened me. Frozen in fear, I lay still. I knew that an animal had been following me.

Was this it? Will it take me now?

I was shocked when a Golden Retriever came running through the bushes, his tail wagging. He came to me and gently licked my face. I slowly sat up, amazed when a man suddenly appeared. I had given up hope of being found alive. I could not believe my eyes.

"Are you Kelly?"

Fear surfaced. *Is he real? Is he from the house that I ran from?* His voice scared me, jarring me from the isolation I had lived in for so many days. My mind was wondering *is he from the good side or the bad side?*

"Who are you? Who are you with?" My voice was weak … and I knew it came out with fear as I said each word.

His voice was calm and gentle. He lowered himself and sat by me. My four-legged angel cuddled up to me and stayed close, reminding me that this was real with each lick of her tongue. "Kelly, my name is Greg and I'm with Search and Rescue. We've been searching for you for five days. We were just about to quit searching for you."

Reaching for his walkie-talkie, I heard him say, "We found Kelly. We are at the side of river …."

As I heard his words, I was stunned that others had been searching for me.

Finally realizing that help had arrived, I asked, "How did you know where to look?" He explained that Thomas had reported me missing and someone came across my car in the ditch. The sheriff's department in Grand County ran the plate and found it belonged to me. With that information, I was formally declared lost.

Crying with happiness, I hugged the dog.

Over a dozen rescue workers were involved. My bloody footprints were discovered and they had been tracking my movements.

Crying with happiness, I hugged the dog, who licked my face again.

"Thank you for finding me," I whispered to my rescuer as I nuzzled the dog's neck. It was so wonderful to see this fur-faced angel. I missed my four-legged boys so much.

"I can't believe it … that you found me," I said, tears running down my cheeks.

"You must be really hungry. Do you want something to eat?"

"Yes, please. I am so hungry. I haven't eaten for many days," was all I could say.

Unzipping his backpack, he fished out a Nature's Way granola bar, handing it to me. I grabbed for the bar. With amazing strength, I ripped open the green wrapper, taking my first bite of food since Hazel landed in the ditch. It tasted amazing. I swear the oats and honey just melted on my tongue. I devoured the bar, so grateful for the food, help, and his presence.

Greg then asked, "Are you hurt? Can you move?"

"I can't walk. I can't even stand." I pointed to my feet.

He took out his first aid kit and said, "It will help to wrap your feet and start warming them up." Putting moleskin on the bottoms of my feet, he then pulled out thick, warm socks and covered them. What I didn't know was that the wrong thing had been put on my feet. When the moleskin was removed, it stripped and shredded what little skin remained.

Two more search-and-rescue guys came walking through the bushes as Greg tended to my feet. One approached, asking, "Are you okay? Do you have broken bones or anything else we can help with?"

"I have frostbite on my feet, and I can't stand or walk. I don't think I have any broken bones. I don't think my feet can be saved."

He replied, "We have an ambulance waiting at a trailhead parking lot to get you to a hospital where you'll be taken care of."

 Greg said to me, "Your brother, Roger, and Thomas are at the command center, but only one can come to help get you out. Which one do you want to see?"

Gaining energy from knowing that I was rescued, I wondered, *Why are they asking me if I want to see Roger or Thomas?* Of course, I would want to see Thomas over anyone else right now.

Little did I know that my rescuers were in protection mode … of me. If I had been in the forest because I was escaping from an abusive situation, they weren't going to put me back in one. At that time, I didn't realize that a spouse was always the first suspect if there was foul play.

Immediately, I replied, "Thomas." I could not wait to see him, my best friend and partner. He had rescued me! I could not believe this was happening and true! Thomas was here and I would get to see him. I was grateful Roger was there and would be so happy to see him, too, but now, my heart was bursting in anticipation of seeing and being with Thomas.

One of the search-and-rescue guys said to me, "My name is Matthew. Greg is going to help you **How did I get down there in the first place?** stand up and help you climb onto my back. I will carry you up the ravine. It's quite steep. We will get you to a flat section where a stretcher will be and you can lay down again.

"Do you think you are strong enough to get on my back if I get down low and Greg helps?"

He looked to be in his early twenties, strong and fit, with well-defined muscles … capable of carrying my almost-lifeless body. "I think I can hold on, but I'm so weak. I'll try."

I wrapped my arms around his neck. It was difficult to hold on to Matthew as he labored up the steep mountain. I did not think I could hold on much longer but sheer willpower kicked in and I used the last of my energy to cling to his back.

It took an unbearably long time to arrive at the top. They laid me on the ground in the shade of a tree on the steep rugged mountainside. As I look up into the tree, I thought, *Is this really real? Am I safe? Could this really be over?*

I was overwhelmed with all the activity … the voices and the movements of Matthew and Greg. When I saw the ravine that had to be climbed up and out of, I wondered how I got down there in the first place. The pitch of it was scary. Then sleep overtook me once again, while my furry friend stayed by my side.

thirty-three
Rescued

Everywhere my bloody footprints were found, bear prints were seen.

Thomas was frustrated. He had to stay at the command center during the day hours. Each evening, he would drive down the mountain, returning home to feed and walk Bob and Boomer, our boxers who we've always called "the boys."

The team had reassured him that it was not a "recovery" yet—finding a body. They were hopeful and in full rescue operation. There were several ATVs that went out each day with a dozen plus on the team. On the last day, the team was down to one ATV. Each morning, Thomas would attend the planning session for the day and then go to the command center and wait for any news.

Mosquitoes were out and Thomas was worried how I was doing. He knew from experience that if mosquitoes were around, I was sure to get bitten extensively. He remembered the itchy nickel- and dime-size welts I would get and imagined I was probably covered with bites over my entire body.

I had left on a Tuesday and Thomas reported me missing on Thursday. A BOLO was put out but my car was not found until the following Thursday, when the official search and rescue operation began, eight days after I'd been missing.

On Friday, my footprints were discovered. There was concern. My footprints contained blood. They also knew that I was barefoot. Every time my bloody footprints were found, bear prints were seen. The team was able to track my bloody prints to the steep ravine.

Matthew returned to the command center to let them know I was found, and to direct the gurney designed for trails. It had a large, thick rubber wheel in the middle, and sidebars that prevented the rescued from falling out.

Waiting, I drifted in and out of consciousness.

The deputy sheriff approached Thomas to tell him that I was found alive. Exhausted, he dropped to his knees and wept with joy.

Greg told me that the search-and-rescue party would be here within an hour with the gurney to transport me off the mountain.

Waiting, I drifted in and out of consciousness, looking up at blue skies and forest trees that surrounded me, in disbelief that I was being rescued and would live.

I heard Thomas calling my name, "Kelly, are you okay?" I sat up and saw him walking toward me. "I can't believe that you found me. I thought I was going to die. That I would never see you again!" I said, crying.

"I'm so glad we found you. They were just calling off the search when we found out you had been seen." We hugged each other, both of us crying now. "I missed you so much. Thank you for finding me … I love you so much!"

"I love you, sweetheart. You're going to be okay."

"Are Paige and Ryan okay? Do they know I've been found and I am alive? They must be so scared; I need to see them."

"I called them and they will be meeting us at the hospital. They are so relieved and can't wait to see you."

"Thomas, my feet are so bad with frostbite, I don't think they can be saved." Tears began to flow.

Thomas wrapped his arms around me, saying, "Don't worry, sweetheart, you are alive and that's all that matters."

My brother stood nearby with a smile on his face and looking relieved. "Kelly, I'm so glad you're safe. Why did you leave and not tell anyone? In his typical funny sarcasm, he added, "This is one heck of a way to lose twenty pounds."

I was happy to see him and to know that he had been searching for me.

Suddenly, I was lifted onto the one-wheel trail gurney. There were more people—the number around me was shocking. Five men, including my brother Roger and one woman from the search-and-rescue team, as well as Thomas, surrounded the gurney. Everyone was smiling and said how happy they were that I was found.

They held onto the sides to steady it as they moved it over rocks and kept it from tipping over. Several from the team went ahead of our litter and tied ropes into trees to further harness the gurney and me as we made our way over the vertical rocky terrain.

I was astonished that I had been found. I looked at my rescuers, forever etching that moment in time in my memory, my heart filled with gratitude.

It was shocking to be back in the real world. Transporting me across the mountain took about 90 minutes. I stared up at the tall pine trees as the cot bounced over the rocks, silently praying, and giving thanks that I had been found. When we finally arrived at the campground where the search-and-rescue command center was stationed, an EMT and ambulance driver were waiting.

With another hug from Thomas, and his promise to meet me at the hospital, I was lifted onto the ambulance stretcher and moved inside. As the doors were closed, I immediately felt anxious, confined, like a trapped bird, scared of what was going to happen when I arrived at the hospital.

Were the doctors going to amputate my feet?

It was shocking to be back in the real world. My senses were reeling with stimulation from my new surroundings. Surprisingly, I found myself wishing I could be back on the mountain, to be alone, back in nature in the rugged beauty of the mountains and pines. I felt like I was leaving a part of me behind.

Remembering that I had been told there were two sides in this battle when I had been taken, I was frightened. *Were all these people on the right side?* I felt overcome by anxiety and worry as I stared out the back windows of the ambulance racing along Highway 40 and then I-70. A young woman EMT began taking my vital signs. Amazingly, my blood pressure and pulse were within normal range!

thirty-four
Reunited

I continued screaming loudly,
unable to move and eventually passed out.

The ambulance arrived at the hospital, which looked like a ski chalet from the outside. They had really captured the mountain feel with the wood beam architecture and inviting entrance. It appeared to be a newer building, a facility that had been updated in 2005.

Upon entering the St. Anthony Summit Medical Center, I was overwhelmed with all the lights … and people. I was amazed that my family was there. Thomas's and Paige's faces displayed relief when they saw me. I burst into tears of gladness.

Paige held my hand. "Oh, Mom, I've been so worried about you. What happened? I love you so much, Mom. I've missed you so much!" as tears rolled down her cheeks.

I was overwhelmed with love when I saw her.

I could see her eyes running up and down my body. "You've lost so much

The darkness and fear … the terror was over.

weight, and your eyes look so large! I'm just so happy you've been found that you're safe, that you are okay," she repeatedly said as she held my hand.

Thomas held my other hand, telling me, "You're safe and you're going to be all right."

Crying in happiness, their hands holding mine tightly, I was still in disbelief that my wish had come true. I had dreamed and imagined how it would feel to see them, and how I would hold them and tell them I loved them so. And here I was, this was real. The darkness and fear ... the terror was over.

I had survived the extreme exposure and trauma, the ongoing threats lurking in the darkness of the night. It was a miracle I was here ... I knew it. For the first time, I felt like I could finally relax and feel safe.

 A tall distinguished-looking man appeared next to my bed and asked me what happened. With penetrating blue eyes staring intensely at me, I told him the basics of what happened: that I got lost when I started walking from my car. He nodded in approval and walked away. I never knew who he was. And he never heard the whole story ... my experience with Heaven and Hell. I don't think he cared.

I learned later that when a person goes missing as I did, authorities must discern if there was a crime committed, or a possible abduction. Was he some kind of investigator?

My fear and distrust had begun to take hold of me. Who was this man? I never heard his name. And I did not know who I should tell of my experience. I decided I would share more details later, but not now ... not to anyone that I didn't know.

I was wheeled into an emergency room with my family at my side. A doctor dressed in a surgical gown and his nurse assistant came to my side. He said he would tend to my frostbitten feet.

A nurse inserted an IV into the vein on my arm and then a vial of morphine as I lay there overcome with joy being with my family once again. Slowly, I felt the numbing that the drug introduced.

As the drug's effect increased, I wondered if I would be able to keep my feet. The doctor was casual as he spoke to me and

I screamed in sheer agony from the pain of the removal.

removed the blanket covering my legs. He began removing the socks and moleskin that had been applied when I was first found.

Immediately, I screamed in sheer agony from the pain of the removal. The sticky moleskin had adhered to my cut and frostbitten flesh. Moleskin should not have been near my skin for the type of injuries I sustained. I remembered looking at my feet on rescue day—lacerated, blistered, and blackened up to my ankles.

I tried to get away from the torture I was experiencing—a pain beyond anything I had endured. The nurses countered my moves and held me down on the hospital bed as I kicked and tried to get away. Thomas kept saying, "Give her something … give her more morphine."

The other nurse pumped more morphine into the IV, and the doctor said, "This will soon be over. We can't give her any more morphine."

It was an excruciating pain as my flesh was pulled away with the glue on the wraps. I continued screaming loudly, unable to move, and I eventually passed out as they worked on my feet, which felt like an eternity.

The fluorescent lights reminded me of my time in Hell and intense fear engulfed my mind again, remembering the horror of what I had gone through and seen before I blacked out from the extreme pain I just had been put through.

thirty-five
The Best News

*As I lay there, the extreme level of pain
radiating from my feet had subsided.*

I awoke in a dimly lit hospital room, alone and scared, feeling
claustrophobic at being confined. It was still a shock to be here …
in the hospital. I did not think I would survive or be found, yet
here I was. I had no idea how long I had slept. My last memory
was screaming in pain in the surgery room before the darkness
fell around me.

As I lay there, the extreme level of pain radiating from my feet
had subsided. At least I could tolerate it. A new threshold of pain
was present. My back was burning in deep pain.

No one was in the room with me. I had no idea what the time
was and didn't know where Thomas was. Looking down at my
legs, I didn't know what was there. I sat up and pulled the sheet
off my feet, although I was afraid of what I would see.

To my relief, both my feet were heavily wrapped in white bandages
… only black toes were sticking out. Counting each toe, I was
relieved that all ten were still there! They looked like black sticks,
with black toenails, barely recognizable as toes, and the flesh was
shriveled.

Leaning back on the bed, I cringed with pain as soon as contact was made. The hospital gown was stuck to my back. Groaning, I sat up and found the button to ring for help.

I had to pee so badly, and I could not get up from the bed. In just a few minutes, a young nurse came and asked if I was okay. She was very kind and had a calm, gentle manner. Telling her I needed help to go to the bathroom and I did not know if I could walk, she brought a wheelchair to the side of the bed and helped me sit in it, then wheeled it to the bathroom in my room.

With her help to stand, l leaned on her arm and managed to sit on the toilet. It was unreal to feel the seat beneath me, a comfort for which I was so grateful. After relieving myself, we made it back to the hospital bed. Sitting back in the wheelchair had irritated my back and it felt on fire like when I was being whipped and beaten in Hell.

I told the nurse that I needed something for my back. Oozing sores stuck to the gown and hurt so badly. She asked me to remove the gown so she could see. She flinched back in surprise when she saw my injuries. "How did you injure your back? You have open cuts on your back, and it's covered with bruises and welts."

"I guess when I slid on my back down the mountain, and crawling over the rocks I scraped it." I never told anyone about the beating I had received when I was in Hell.

Changing me into a fresh gown and rubbing ointment on my back, she asked, "Would you like something to eat?"

"I cannot wait to eat. I don't know how long I was lost but I haven't eaten in days. I would love something to eat … thank you so much." And I was truly grateful. I was hungry.

She handed me the food menu. It was hard to choose something … there was so much to choose from. I wanted everything. Here was all the food that I had dreamed of eating. I should get something healthy, I thought, but ordered a burger and fries. I was looking forward to my first meal in almost two weeks.

I ate that meal like nobody's business. Taking a big bite of my cheeseburger, it was delicious, and I savored dipping the salty fries in ketchup. I had thought I would eat the whole burger, but my stomach had shrunk, and I quickly felt full. It was the best meal I ever had. I was so happy that I could look forward to another meal.

I called the nurse when I was finished. She asked how I was feeling and then said, "You must have been so frightened at being lost."

It was an open-ended statement. She wanted to hear more, and I felt I could trust her. Then, I started talking, telling her that there were other dimensions that people cannot see. That there were good and bad forces, and that if people did not turn to God and Jesus, obey God's commandments, that God's wrath would be terrifying when it came down. When I revealed that there would be a zombie apocalypse, her face filled with alarm. I knew she believed me when I shared my information. I told her that I, too, was afraid.

As I spoke, she was rubbing ointment on my back. She then said, "We have a chapel here. You could go to it if you wanted. There are ministers and priests that come to visit patients." If I wanted, I could request a visit. There were also services I could attend.

The second night, Paige stayed with me, and I told her what had happened, in as much detail as I could remember. How I first became lost. I did omit the Heaven and Hell part, not wanting to scare her. I told her I had missed her and thought of her the whole time I was gone. I was so happy to have my daughter there.

I could see she was traumatized, and I didn't want to cause her more worry. I did not realize how profoundly my disappearance had affected her. She told me she had been so scared, and just minutes before receiving Thomas' phone call that I had been found, she had broken down crying, praying, and begging God to bring me home.

I'm sure God heard and answered her prayers. I don't think it was a coincidence. I was so grateful for her love and to be together again as we held each other that night.

Receiving attentive and tender care, I felt like all the nurses and doctors were angels. A new doctor came in to talk to me about what happened. As he spoke, he unwrapped the bandages that had covered my feet. My left foot was more injured than the right and they were concerned I might lose a few toes.

I received the good news that overall, my feet would recover. I would have to have surgery to sew up the torn flesh and fatty tissue and remove the dead flesh on the bottoms of my feet to help them heal.

Several times a day, the nurses would rub colloidal silver ointment on my feet. They were very gentle in tending to my injuries. The doctor said I was very lucky I had been found that day because my feet may not have recovered had they been exposed any longer.

I had my first shower. It was strange to be doing the things that I had always taken for granted. It felt amazing to feel warm water on the front of my body and wash my hair. I was stunned when I first saw my reflection in the bathroom mirror. My eyes looked huge in my deeply tanned face, my cheekbones were protruding, and my face looked so thin, as if my flesh had shrunk. The look in my eyes was wild, scared, like a trapped animal.

I had lost 20 pounds and looked lean, more muscular. I was not overweight before but would have liked to lose 10-15 pounds, so the weight loss was okay with me. I just wished it had not happened in this way. My hair was shiny and smooth, more lustrous than I remembered. My body was a deep golden-brown from all my time warming my body in the sun on the rocks. Strange, I had no bug or spider bites. Everyone scratched their heads as to why my body and face weren't covered with any bites.

The lights were disturbing, reminding me of the hell room where I was beaten.

Looking over my shoulder, I saw my whipped back. It looked like a vicious flogging had drawn blood. There was deep purple, red, and yellow discoloration around the welts, now beginning to crust over in scabs where my flesh had been torn. It would heal. But for now, I was in misery.

The sight scared me as I remembered Hell and I did not feel safe anymore. Everything felt weird. Being around so many people was overwhelming. The lights were disturbing, reminding me of the Hell room where I was beaten. I missed being in nature. In a strange way I longed to be in the woods again—almost as if it was calling to me.

I had never seen my son cry as he was doing now when he came to the hospital. All I could say as I held his hand was, "I'm so happy to see you. I'm so sorry for everything. I love you. I missed you so much. I thought I would never see you again!"

My sister Jayne, Ted, and Aunt Bernadette had driven up the mountain with Ryan and some of my cousins showed up. Each expressed their happiness that I had been found. It meant a lot that they had made the trip up the mountain to visit me. With tears and hugs, and well wishes, I felt loved by my family. They were so dear to me, and I had thought about them so many times as I had looked at our family pictures.

Thomas drove up in the morning. He said news reporters were wanting to interview me. My ordeal made national news. A local news station interviewed us both. Thomas spoke with *KUSA*, the *NBC* affiliate, and *KMGH*, the *ABC* affiliate, asked for a meeting if I was up for it. I agreed to an interview and signed papers allowing them to film their questions and my answers.

I trusted that Thomas said it would be okay to talk to them. I did not know what to expect when the camera crew came into my hospital room. The news reporter asked, "Why did you go to the mountains?"

My response was, "I was going for a day trip, to have some alone time and meditate in the mountains. I had been trying to sort out personal issues …." I also told him that Reiki had saved me and my feet. I could not tell him the real reason, that the Voice had led me here.

No one was especially interested in Reiki and pretty much ignored what I said. After endless questions and filming my feet, feet—that's what the camera person wanted to focus on—they left. Some of the interview segments and a flash on my wounded feet would air on local television.

Most of their questions were stupid … as in why did I get lost? *Really?!*

Why didn't I tell anyone that I was leaving my car?

Battery in the car was dead. I had no phone. I didn't know how to telepath my thoughts.

I stayed in the hospital for three nights. Paige stayed one night with me, sleeping on a small couch in the room. Thomas drove back and forth, staying with our dogs at night, then back to be with me. Overall, the reaction from others, strangers that heard

I became almost a recluse.

about my ordeal, were supportive. But there were some negative criticisms, where I was accused of being stoned on marijuana or just stupid.

I agreed with some of the disparaging remarks. It appeared extremely foolish to not tell anyone where I was going, especially a trip to the mountains. I had made a mistake in leaving my car and the space blanket for sure.

Thomas was careful to keep me shielded from the backlash on social media that were scathing and mean toward me. One of the pictures that had been given to the media by a family member showed me with a drink in hand, looking a little tipsy at a family party and that image probably did not help how I was perceived. Not surprisingly, it's the one that was reprinted. It wasn't who I was.

Few knew how I withdrew from the outside. I became almost a recluse.

thirty-six

Forever Changed

*What I had experienced and survived
was just a taste of what was to come.*

The following morning, a Catholic priest came to my room. I felt relief when he walked in and said, "Good morning." He asked me a few questions, calmly asking me about my religious beliefs. I responded that I was a Christian and believed in Jesus.

I then told him, "I am scared for myself and my family. That we needed to be blessed and protected from evil. What I saw in Hell, I now knew that demons were real. It's not Hollywood … it is the truth."

What I didn't tell him was what was flowing through my mind.

And the house, whatever was going on at the house that was causing chaos and trouble, I would soon be going home to. I needed to hear that everything would be all right … for me … for all of us.

Before he came into the room, I had looked at myself in the bathroom mirror. My face expressed terror; I looked like a wild child. I think he saw it … maybe he felt it. He told me, "You have already been anointed and were protected. Your family will be okay as well."

We prayed the Lord's Prayer together. Once again, he anointed me, making the sign of the cross as he told me, "My daughter, have faith and believe in the saving grace of our Lord, Jesus Christ."

I could not tell him what had really happened, but his loving presence and prayers brought me comfort. I could feel my face and body relaxing with his presence.

Immediately, I slipped to my knees.

I maneuvered my body off my hospital bed into the wheelchair and wheeled myself down the hallway toward the chapel the nurse had told me about.

There was no one there. Absorbing the quietness, I wheeled to the closest pew and transitioned to sit on it. Immediately, I slipped to my knees, my forearms resting on the bench in front of me and my hands were joined in prayer.

Tears slipped out of my eyes as I prayed in gratitude for being found. As I prayed, I revealed to God that I felt confused and bewildered. I was overwhelmed and scared and filled with a deep sense of knowing that my life had been forever changed. And that I did not know what to do with the new knowledge that I had … knowledge that I had received when I was being pulled between Heaven and Hell.

Wheeling back to my room, the hallway felt longer and narrower than I remember it. When I got to the confinement of my room, the walls were closing in. I missed the forest, the openness and fresh air, but I did not miss the darkness, in the evening hours when I could not see my hands in front of my eyes.

As I thought of my ordeal, fear erupted. I never wanted to be in the darkness again. The lights had to be left on. I longed for the peace and love of Heaven, where I was safe. I needed someone to help me, guide me. I felt so alone and knew that someone … something was controlling "the Game" I had been sucked into.

The world I once knew was now turned upside down. My time in the hospital went by fast. Over the four days, my body was slowly healing, but I was overwhelmed by all that had happened. I realized that God had a purpose for me, a purpose for all of us, a plan of salvation we all had a part in.

Life had been tough, traumatic, and would become even more so. What I had experienced and survived was just a taste of what was to come.

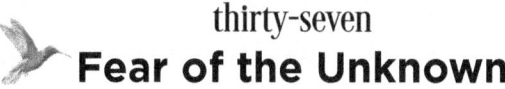

thirty-seven

Fear of the Unknown

There was so much sensory input,
I suddenly felt a jolt of fear.

The four days in the hospital went by fast. I left in a wheelchair, feet bandaged with protective boots and a lot of cuts and scrapes covered my legs but otherwise in good physical shape, although mentally not so intact. The healthcare professionals were focused on my feet and little else. No one ever seemed concerned or curious about what I was feeling emotionally or mentally. I just went home. I was started back on my medications and given pain pills to take home with me.

Paige remembered when a newspaper photographer showed up to take pictures of my feet. Thomas had told the press that I was not available to **The city looked alien.** them. A reporter showed up when he was not there and told Paige that her father had approved it.

The reporter asked me, "What led you to the mountains?" My response was odd. I told him that the earth was dying and we need to save the trees. It seemed reasonable to me at the time.

I was unhinged in much of what I said and thought. Little did I know how deep my trauma was. And it was my family that would deal with it for years to come.

It was surreal to find myself sitting in our car and driving along the highway, headed home. The city looked alien with all the buildings, skyscrapers, traffic, and people. There was so much sensory input, I suddenly felt a jolt of fear. The world as I understood it was so different now. I knew that there were two sides at play, with no playbook.

I was clueless about how to play this Game I had been in for the last few months, but so incredibly happy to be back with my family.

When I entered the house, Bob and Boomer were dancing around, tails wagging. Their presence was healing to my sense of well-being. I could sense they understood me and my fears and were always beside me as I convalesced, loving and guarding.

That night after Thomas had cared for me, the house settled down. My back still was painful. It would be a long time before I could sleep on it. Thomas was a restless sleeper and settled in the spare room for the night.

My memory was vague as to what happened next and why I did it. For Thomas, it was crystal clear, even over a decade later. I disappeared.

Holy shit … where is she? I just got her back and she's gone again.

The next morning Thomas found me asleep in a nearby park, under a big evergreen with my walker close by. I woke to his words, "Honey … sweetheart … what are you doing here in the park?"

"I wanted to be outside."

"We gotta get you home. You can't sleep in the park," was his response. I didn't want to go.

Thomas lovingly cared for me, changing my bandages several times a day and bathing my feet. I was so afraid to have my feet touched and winced when he applied the colloidal silver, but I must admit it was endearing. Soon, I came to enjoy his loving touch, especially as my flesh mended and the pain subsided.

Life was busy for him: cooking; shopping; walking Bob and Boomer; taking care of my feet; helping me bathe; and juggling his full-time job. Luckily, his employer allowed him to work from home and he was always just a call away. The meals he cooked and served were plentiful, a mini-feast each time. I was always so grateful for each meal and gave thanks to God.

Paige and Ryan would come into my room and visit for a while. It was always so uplifting to see their faces, to be alive and present in their lives. As I was recovering, lying in bed, Ryan came into the room with his acoustic guitar and played several songs that brought tears to my eyes. I felt really happy to be there with him. This was a big treat, a memory of a lifetime.

A few days after we returned home, Hazel was dropped off at our house. Mom's friend owned a towing company and sent his largest tow truck, used for towing semis, with a painted-on logo of the Denver Broncos horse. It lifted her out of the ditch, and someone had added new tires to Hazel.

When I was discharged from the hospital, I was on my own—and so was my family. We left with instructions to follow up with my internal medicine doctor. I found out just how bad my condition was. I had been treated for renal failure, tachycardia, exposure, hyponatremia (causes confusion and possible coma), frostbite, and rhabdomyolysis (a breakdown of skeletal muscle). None of the hospital professionals expressed any concern about the trauma I had endured or the status of my mental health.

I knew I would not have lasted another day and felt lucky to be alive. I knew that when I was lying by the river and mentally talking to Grandma that I was at my end, that I was dying.

Thomas knew I would need a foot doctor. I wasn't surprised. I was given a referral to a foot doctor to see the day after I was discharged. The doctors still weren't sure if I would lose toes or if my feet would fully recover.

I was extremely anxious about anyone touching my feet. The painful memory of the doctor pulling the moleskin off was too fresh in my mind. Kenneth Morgan, MD, came into my life. He was compassionate and gentle when he examined my feet and gave me the good news that I could look forward to full healing and keeping all my toes!

With a scalpel, he sliced off a piece of damaged tissue for the lab to analyze before surgery. The result was a searing, burning pain that vibrated from the bottom of my foot, through my ankle, and settled in my mid-calf.

The following week I had foot surgery to remove the dead flesh and fat. Dr. Morgan sewed up my feet, leaving a scar that looked like a bear paw on the bottom of my left foot and a smaller scar on the bottom of my right. He forewarned me that when I began walking, it would feel like walking on my hands with bare knuckles. When I'm barefoot, he was right. I was now confined to a wheelchair for several weeks with my legs extended.

A few days after my surgery, I watched in stunned silence as the closet door

I sat terrified as he pulled open the closet door.

handle started turning left and right several times, making a clicking noise as I lay in bed. It was as if something was in the closet trying to open the door to get out.

I called for Thomas, yelling at him to hurry, telling him something was in the closet. I sat terrified as he quickly pulled open the closet door, revealing nothing inside but clothes hanging on the racks and shoes on the floor.

With dread, I watched the closet door handle whenever I was in bed, but it never moved again or made the clicking sound. It only took one time to drive home that I was being haunted or hunted by evil.

I felt the presence was always there ... watching and listening.

Whatever this energy or spirit was that had followed me in the forest was now here ... in my home. I felt the presence was always there ... watching and listening. I knew that there are other dimensions present and invisible to the eye. It was relentless. The Game was still on, the Voice echoing in my mind telling me I had to compete against a force I could not see and a series of challenges that only I knew about.

The outdoors continued to call to me. Still confined to my wheel-chair, I slipped out of the house in the middle of the night, not telling anyone where I was going. Moving the wheelchair forward with my arms on the wheels, I made my way out the front door and down the sidewalk for several blocks. The neighborhood park was my destination, and I spent the night beneath one of the trees. I asked and, as usual, never received an answer as to why I needed to do this.

As I made my way back to the house at dawn, I could see Thomas standing out on the sidewalk looking for me. He ran down the sidewalk and over to me. "What happened? Why did you leave?"

Again, my response for my odd behavior was, "I wanted to be outside with the trees and I missed the forest."

There was a part of me that longed to be back on the mountain, to answer the call and to just sit and be a part of the forest, this time with shoes.

Over the next few weeks, I had little bits of guidance with the help of others. My Aunt Bernadette and her friend Edna heard what happened and came to visit, bringing a rosary, prayer cards, and a Pieta prayer book filled with Catholic prayers. I had never prayed a rosary. I'd only seen my grandmother with rosary beads in her hands quite often, but I learned it quickly.

It felt good to be alive!

Edna was in her fifties. She was a kind, devout Catholic, and a live-ly, fun person to be around. She asked if I would like to spend an evening with her and a neighborhood friend that was like a son to her. Thomas was against it. He thought I should be home but I convinced him I would be okay and he would know where I was. I was drawn to Edna's positivity and happy spirit and looking forward to learning more about her faith.

On a hot summer afternoon in July, she picked me up with my wheelchair in a very old, beat-up truck. With windows rolled down we sped along Interstate 25. She was a fast driver and whipped that old truck in and out of traffic like an expert. It felt good to be alive!

Edna and I sat out on her porch talking about her job, the places she had traveled as an airline stewardess, her church, her neighborhood, and the young man she mentored who was like a son to her. After eating a lamb chop, baked potato, and asparagus spears, I reclined in a lazy boy with my bandaged feet raised.

Suddenly, Edna came into the room, holding a baseball bat in her hands. Smacking the top of the bat into her opposite hand, she appeared menacing. In my state of mind, I was spooked and I thought about the movie *Misery* with Kathy Bates as the overzealous fan who smashes James Caan with a bat, breaking his feet.

I wondered if she saw fear in my eyes as she gently placed the bat on the floor. I pointed to a large statue of an angel with wings. It was as large as a human and holding a rod in its hand, standing over a serpent. I asked who the angel was. Edna said this was Archangel Michael and he battled Satan and won, the most powerful of all angels.

I've heard of angels but didn't know much about them. I asked her, "What are they battling over?"

She replied, "Archangel Michael is sent by God to help humanity."

Later she showed me her St. Michael rosaries that were beautifully colored crystal beads. She said it would be good to pray to St. Michael daily because he warded off evil. He was the leader of the army of God and the leader of Heaven's forces in their triumph over the powers of hell. It was a lifeline to me, invaluable advice to receive help from this protective and healing angel.

That was music to my ears, something useful and helpful for my situation. I knew I needed all the help I could get and would pray for his help. In the Pieta prayer book she had given me there was a "Prayer to Defeat the Work of Satan." A footnote that followed says, "God governs the world but prayer governs God." I became a prayer warrior from then on.

My Reiki teacher heard what happened and visited a few times to see how I was and gave me Reiki on my feet. She was so calming and gentle, a very spiritual person. I could not feel anything like I used to feel with the energy flowing in my feet. It was as if the flow had just stopped.

She brought along another teacher, Charlie, a person I had known years ago. He had seen the news article about me being lost and was a great healer. He knew about trauma and healing and introduced me to EFT ... the Emotional Freedom Technique. We spent many afternoons talking and tapping points on our bodies while saying affirmations.

Although I was grateful for Reiki, it seemed that I was no longer attuned to the energy flow. I wondered if my time in the other dimensions had changed my healing vibration. I found it difficult now to give self-Reiki.

Now, my feet were blocked due to the frostbite.

thirty-eight

The Secret Continues

It was humanity at its worst.

OMG ... I'm hearing the Voice once more. I was being called to go places again. I felt like a puppet, being controlled by something I didn't understand.

This time I loaded up my car with provisions: food, water, clothes, pillows, blankets, my prayer books, and rosary. I had no destination in mind ... just to drive north for a few hours. I would be back by early afternoon.

I ended up in Laramie, Wyoming, and visited the University of Wyoming, a two-hour drive from home. There was a sign that referenced where the Mathew Shepard memorial bench was located, and I recalled the brutality and torture that was directed at him and his death when the assailants hung him on a fence to freeze.

It was humanity at its worst. The torture that was inflicted upon him that led to his death was unconscionable. Getting national attention, it was the launch of today's public awareness into hate crimes.

I was surprised that this was where I was led. Although I had feelings of grief of his needless death at the time years ago, I didn't have any other connection to going there. When I arrived, the thought was driven home that hate and violence against anyone was wrong and again God was making this clear to me.

Sitting on the bench I said a prayer. Opening my Bible, the verse from Luke 10: 26-27 came into view:

> He said unto Him, What is written in the law? How readest thou? And He answering said, Thou shalt love the Lord thy God with all thy heart, and with all thy soul, and with all thy strength, and with all thy mind; and thy neighbor as thyself.

I had lost my purse and wallet on the mountain, but I did have a new phone. I'm still oblivious of anything to do with money. I didn't have a credit card or money, only my checkbook. If I wrote a check, it would be paid. My credit cards had been lost in the mountains and were not replaced.

Soon, I realized my gas tank was approaching empty.

Calling Thomas, his response was, "Honey … where are you? Why did you leave? Come back home."

"I'm in Wyoming. I'm low on gas and have no cash. I need you to fill up my tank."

I knew he was frustrated with me. He said, "Let me talk to the station owner to see if he will take my credit card over the phone."

He did, and I was back on my way. Back to where?

Still following the Voice, I found places to hike and make my loops while I prayed for enlightenment and guidance, this time never straying too far from my car. I enjoyed being on the road and the connection

Why should I go?

to the Voice. I felt we had a dialogue with each other. I could hear it … it could hear me. Finally, I heard *You are done …* and I would head back home to Thomas.

The Voice called to me again, urging me back to the mountains. Oh yes, I had fears. A large part of me did not want to go. The thought of being alone in the mountains once again caused anxiety and bad memories crashed in. The darkness, pain, and suffering had happened only two months earlier. The Voice was compelling. I would ask, "Why should I go?" The answer wasn't an answer. The Voice just said, "You have to go … you have to go where I tell you."

I had to continue to do as the Voice asked. Despite my post-traumatic stress and wounded feet, I was called to get back out there making myself vulnerable to both sides. I did not know why.

I knew part of this Game was keeping it secret and heard in my mind that I wouldn't be able to go if I told Thomas that I could hear the Voice and was in the Game. The Voice had told me that I had to keep things secret … that no one could know about it or the Game. Thomas couldn't know.

I was only planning on a two-day trip and rationalized that Thomas seemed to be okay with it … with any of them that I took off on. When I made these, he seemed to have compassion and was patient with me. Sometimes I made it home on my own. Some-times, he had to come get me. I still felt bad that I could not just open up about all that had happened and what I learned.

The secret was causing problems. Would it ever go away?

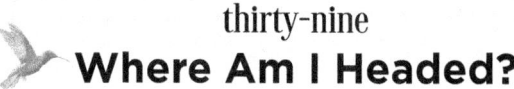

thirty-nine
Where Am I Headed?

Nothingness surrounded me.
It reminded me of the abyss.

It had been 80 days since I had been found on that Father's Day in 2010, and I found myself heading west again. Stopping at Roger's convenience store in Blackhawk, I persuaded the clerk to cash my check, buying food and drinks.

It was dark outside when I took the back road from Bergen Park onto highway 103 to Road 66 and on to Mt. Evans Scenic Byway. I had no clear destination in mind. I had never been to this tourist spot, which I later learned was the highest paved road in North America.

A day trip to the top was a journey that snaked and climbed through nearly 9,000 feet of elevation gain, from the high plains of Denver through five climate zones to the 14,264-foot summit of Mount Evans, one of fifty-eight peaks in Colorado that soar to 14,000 feet and above—one of the famous "fourteeners."

The entrance to the byway was unmanned at the visitor check in. Why wasn't anyone here? The shades were pulled down as I drove past the guard shack and onto a narrow, rutted, and windy two-lane blacktop road with extreme drop-offs.

After a few winding miles through a forested area, the perilous road was now on the side of a sheer cliff wall. Nothingness surrounded me. It reminded me of the abyss. My hands were glued to the wheel, and I tried to ignore the vast darkness that enveloped me. I had just made it to the summit parking lot when snow began to blow sideways.

The Game was in play. My feet were back from the ordeal, still bandaged, but I could get them in hiking books. I was frightened at the drive I had made, and I was here all alone. Again, asking *why* in my head.

I heard my instructions from the Voice. *Now, you have to make a loop.*

Making sure my lights were off and I had my keys, I quickly got out and walked through the parking lot, hiking a small loop and then back to Hazel. It was freezing cold up here as the wind whipped the snowflakes in circles.

The weather and road conditions could change so quickly at high elevation, and I worried the uneven roads might ice up for my treacherous and scary ride back down the mountain. Ice could be dangerous and deadly.

Telling myself not to be scared, I buckled myself in and tried to calm my anxious mind, turning on the radio, distracting myself by singing the lyrics to "Tiny Dancer" by Elton John. I had the impression that whatever was after me could find me if I was fearful. It could sense fear. I was now aware that even my emotions have a frequency. My energy was turning my thoughts to a positive outlook. That I could do.

I drove the 28 miles on the dangerous road and I made it back to the guard shack and entrance to the summit, breathing a huge sigh of relief. Deciding I would sleep in my car, I parked in the Echo Lake parking lot and prayed. I was deeply grateful that I had made it back safely and didn't have to worry anymore about driving off a cliff in the middle of the night. From the lot, I could see the restaurant/gift shop—my next destination in the morning for breakfast.

Settling myself in Hazel in the back where I folded down the seats, I created a comfortable bed with the blankets and pillows and fell into a deep sleep. When I awoke, I was relieved to see I was still the only car parked in the lot.

Excited to explore the trails, I packed up my backpack with water, snacks, and first-aid supplies for my feet. Looking forward to a good breakfast, I turned the key in the ignition. Nothing. It only clicked. The car battery had been losing charge lately and here I was again, stranded.

Leaving my backpack in the car, I started the long walk to Mt. Evans Lodge along the roadway. It was only about a mile up the road but especially long for me because my feet were still bandaged and sore. As I slowly made my way down the highway, a caravan of Harley Davidson motorcycle riders came by, bearing American flags.

A few riders pulled up beside me and asked if I wanted a ride. They were on their way cross-country for a 9/11 memorial. I climbed behind an older gentleman who drove me to the lodge. I was so grateful for the ride. My feet were already burning in pain, and I had only walked about a half mile. I wished him a safe journey and said my prayers were with them.

Going inside, I browsed around the gift shop as I waited for someone to help me. I explained to the manager that my car battery was dead, and I needed a jump-start. Was there anyone that could help me?

The manager was understanding, said it happened all the time and they had an employee who could help me out when he had a break in his shift.

Choosing a rain jacket, ball cap and some tourist souvenirs, the manager rang up my purchase and announced that Robert was now free to help me with my car.

Robert was a shy young guy in his mid-twenties with a friendly smile. We walked out to his car, and he apologized that it was so small. He said his little yellow car was economical and he drove a lot. He shared that at least once every few weeks he was either giving someone a jump-start or using a coat hanger to unlock a door.

After Robert hooked up the car batteries, we sat and talked for a while. He told me he lived in Evergreen and had gone to high school there. Right now, he lived with his grandparents and was trying to save money. I enjoyed chatting with him. He seemed easygoing and reminded me a little of my own children, young and full of dreams.

He offered to make his favorite lunch for me if I came back to the lodge the next day. Saying he had to get back to work, he said he would come back and see if I was still around when he got off work and would bring some beer.

Later that afternoon Robert came back as promised with an ice-cold six-pack of Pabst Blue Ribbon. It was dusk, quickly becoming dark. I handed him one of my two flashlights and we both went in search of wood to build a fire. He returned with tree boughs and pinecones and lit them on fire in the fire grill, blowing hard to make it light.

He said he was an expert at building fires and the trick was to keep blowing air to make it ignite. After the fire was burning brightly, we sat at the picnic table and started talking about him and his family.

Robert revealed he was half Irish, pointing to his red hair, and Choctaw Indian but did not know much about his Indian ancestry. I told him that I had Native American Apache ancestry. I didn't know a lot about the Apache, other than they were a tribe that lived in southwestern Colorado.

He loved to snowboard and had just broken up with his girlfriend who had cheated on him. Then he revealed he had tried to stab her with a pocketknife and ended up going to jail. I felt a jolt of fear and alarm but all I could say was that I was sorry that had happened to him. Then, our conversation turned to supernatural happenings.

I told him some of what happened when I was lost in the mountains, that my feet were heavily bandaged, and it was painful to walk. I didn't include the Heaven and Hell part. The conversation turned scary and strange when he said he had grown up in the Baptist church. He did not believe in God and that when he died, he would be going straight to hell to burn in the eternal fire and sulfur.

"There is no God, only evil, only Satan, the Devil," he said as his voice became louder, huskier and began to change, sounding deep and guttural. He sounded possessed! He scared me.

Anger was permeating from him, and I became very frightened at his sudden change. It seemed that some other force had taken over his body, and he appeared larger and menacing.

I tried to defuse the palpable tension in the air and told him, "Jesus loves all of us, even if we had **You are halfway there.** sinned. Robert, you should have faith, whatever sin you had … ask for forgiveness. God is loving and forgiving." The more I spoke of Jesus, the angrier he became.

I had a sudden Voice message that whatever Robert said to me I had to echo what he said and repeat it in my mind. Had he tapped into my thoughts? As I started repeating in my mind all that he said to me, he told me in a now-normal voice, "You are halfway there." It made me think of a popular song by Bon Jovi. I said I needed to get back to my car and would see him tomorrow.

I knew through the Voice messages I received what I needed to do the next day. I needed to complete my hike and return to Thomas.

After putting out the fire, we walked back to my car, I grabbed a candle, handing it to him and said I would be praying for him and would see him tomorrow for the sandwich he said he would grill for me.

When I was safely back in Hazel and alone, I was left wondering what had just happened. Did he know my thoughts? Were we communicating without speaking? Did I imagine what had just happened? It was all so bizarre.

I felt I needed to do more hiking. I was worried. If "this" was only *halfway there*, what did the other half entail?

Hazel was the only car parked in the lot as I took out the Pieta prayer book and began praying in earnest for guidance and protection from the demons and the dark side of others. I didn't think it was a coincidence that I was here at Echo Lake and had my conversation with Robert. Hopefully, my prayers would reach God and I would be sheltered with His love.

My body slowly relaxed as I felt a sense of calm and peace, and faith that once again, I would be okay. I crawled into the back of Hazel and wrapped myself up in my blankets. A solid night's sleep followed.

forty
Hand of God

Please help me find the trail …

Waking early the next morning, I was elated that my car started and headed to the lodge restaurant. It was loud and super busy when I opened the front door. Large groups of family tourists were enjoying breakfast at long picnic-style wooden tables. There was a good vibe in the restaurant and people sounded happy enjoying themselves.

I chose steak and eggs, with hash browns and toast, thinking I would need a hearty, protein-packed breakfast to give me energy for my upcoming hike. And I asked my server if Robert was there.

A few minutes later, he came to the table, looking happy and harmless … surprised to see me. He asked why I had come so early. I told him I wanted to get going on my hike. He seemed disappointed that he would not be making his favorite Reuben sandwich with the secret Thousand Island dressing for me. There was no mention of our conversation the night before.

As I was finishing the last of my breakfast, Robert came out of the kitchen again. I told him I would come back again sometime and try the Reuben, and we should stay in touch. After chatting for a few minutes, he said the pies were homemade and I should try his favorite: the coconut cream pie. I got the pie to go and promised to keep in touch when he wrote down his contact information.

As I was getting into Hazel, the small slip of paper with Robert's phone number and email blew away in the wind and I never found it. I told myself if I came back here, I would be sure to get his info again.

I parked Hazel at Echo Lake, unsure how far I would hike. In a hurry, I grabbed my backpack with my water bottle and a few snacks and set out with the intention to hike to the Idaho Springs Reservoir.

After hiking through the soft wooded forest trail from the lake, the trail became rockier and began a perilous hike across a sandy ledge about 18-36 inches wide. On one side was a steep 70-degree angle granite cliff. One misstep and I would very likely sustain injuries.

The trail wound down the cliff wall in a series of switchbacks, about a 500-foot decrease in elevation. Then I was at the bottom of the trail with heavy forest and a makeshift bridge to cross the creek.

Just a few hundred feet from the creek, I was at the service road that leads to the reservoir. Fairly steep, the road gains about 300 feet of elevation. Following the mile-long road up to the reservoir, I stopped and wondered if I should turn around. Each step I took was a painful jolt for my feet.

Deciding I would make a loop around the reservoir and head back home, I began walking around the perimeter of the water. I saw something bright that looked like a yellow ball floating in the water.

As I got closer, I saw that it was an apple, and grabbed a stick to get it close enough so I could pluck it out of the water and eat it later.

When I got to the far south side of the lake, the trail disappeared and I was walking in a muddy marsh, my feet soaking wet, mud seeping into my hiking boots.

The reservoir isn't large, and it took me about an hour to make it around the perimeter, ending up at two small cabins, one with a covered deck and chairs. I remembered a time Thomas and I had hiked there in a big thunderstorm with our dogs. We took shelter under that deck and drank out of our thermos filled with hot chicken noodle soup. As we sipped on the soup, Thomas had poured some in the cup to cool and share with them. Of course, they devoured the offering.

Now, taking off my muddy boots, wet socks, and bandages, I washed my feet with water and a cleansing wipe. Wondering the whole time why I was called to come here, I wrapped my swollen red feet in hand towels from my backpack. I gingerly pulled on my boots and made the decision I would walk to the upper lake. Chicago Trail #52 was a popular trail and could be busy on weekends. Today, there was no one around. It had been a beautiful day, with incredible surroundings—the green forest with majestic mountains all around.

Too late, I realized I had left my flashlight in the car. It would take at least three to four hours for me to go back and get it, and I didn't have the energy to start over. The Voice encouraged me to continue on to the summit.

Each step was a searing, burning pain as I slowly hiked past the entrance, deeper into the Mount Evans wilderness area, following the narrow trail. The trail climbed over 600 feet for the next mile, stepping up over rocks and over tree limbs through a burn area, the result of a fire in the 1970s, then continued to climb to Lower Chicago Lake, a total elevation gain of 2,537 feet and a total of 12 miles out and back. The trail passed through steep areas, gaining altitude with massive cliff walls and expansive meadows.

I did not feel afraid of being alone on the mountain and sensed spirits in the woods, maybe Native American spirits or wood fairies. They did not feel malevolent, just watchful.

As I found myself once again listening to the Voice, this felt like a test: spiritual, mental, and physical. I reminded myself, it's not uncommon for me to push myself, competitive in challenging myself to finish what I start.

I will finish this and be fine, I told myself.

It was early dusk when I scrambled up the steep boulders leading to Upper Chicago Lake. In my mind I heard the Voice say, *They call this the Hand of God.* It did feel as if I was in the palm of God's hand, when I looked at the expanse of the mountains, forest, and lakes, here at this altitude, words were not enough to say how beautiful was God's creation.

Now I had to force myself to loop the upper lake. I was so tired. It had been taxing to make the final steep ascent to the lake. I wanted to turn around here, and say I made it to the summit, but the lake beckoned me—one more loop.

The day was on the cusp of turning into night when I made my way down the mountain. I felt redeemed somehow that I had kept my word and looped the mountain, but I needed to get out of the lake area where it was hard to follow the trail.

It was so heavily wooded that very little light shone through, and the path was tricky to follow. I had a pretty good sense of direction, awareness of myself relative to my location, and clear memory of twists and turns of the trail but I knew here in the thick of the woods I could become lost.

It was now pitch-black on the mountain, but I had made my way out of the heavy woods. Relieved to be back on the trail, I cried tears of relief. The narrow trail traveled in a mostly straight line back down the mountain to the trailhead and service road and would be easy to follow if I stayed on the path.

The stars were brilliant, and moonlight reflected off some of the rocks on the trail. At times, they almost looked like stepping stones glowing in the night. It's strange how my perception of everything changed in darkness.

Why was this happening to me *again*?

I could not believe that I was in the dark again.
I couldn't believe I left the flashlight in the car.

At least I had boots and warm clothes on, and I was not lost. I had hiked this mountain enough to feel confident I could make it back to the road, even in the dark. I knew where I was.

What was it?

Going so slowly, it felt like I would never get to the trailhead. I felt joyous and a rush of adrenaline to be back at the service road, and seeing the small cabins was such a glorious sight. I continued walking the mile back to the trailhead down the wide dirt road.

I couldn't see the wooden trail marker sign in the dark. It was difficult to spot, even in the day. I was becoming desperate and panicked. I just wanted to get back to Hazel.

I prayed, *Oh, my dear God, please help me find the trail.*

In the black of the night, a pair of large round red eyes appeared, emitting a glowing light for three to four seconds. Oh, what the hell was that? I was frightened as I stared into the dark forest, with the pair of red eyes glowing again.

Thank you, thank you for helping me!

What was that? "It" created just enough illumination that I could see the trail marker that it stood next to. Whatever the creature was, it was about four feet tall. I could not make out a body shape or see its face.

Grateful for this help, I followed the glowing red eyes that would flash about every five feet ahead of me, lighting the trail all the way, at least 20 or so times, across the bridge over the creek, and up the steep rocky switchbacks.

I was so intent on getting off the mountain, I had lost my fear of the creature, whatever it was. It was guiding me through the darkness. Out loud, I cried, "Thank you, thank you for helping me!"

I could almost ignore the horrible pain in my feet as my adrenaline kicked in full gear in anticipation of the trail ledge with the treacherous drop-off that I would have to cross to get back to Echo Lake.

I never saw the creature with the glowing red eyes again once I reached the narrow ledge.

Now, I was less than a mile from Hazel, with the worst behind me. I was completely exhausted and amazed I had made it.

It was almost midnight when I reached Hazel. I was way too tired to drive home and would have to sleep here in the parking lot once again. I had won the test.

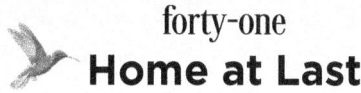

forty-one
Home at Last

I know I must have looked as beat as I felt.

The next day I woke up in agony. My feet were on fire with shooting and dull throbbing pain. I felt old with arthritic fatigue and sore muscles, but it was worth it, and I was happy it was behind me. Now, I could go home.

Limping, I stumbled to the outhouse to relieve myself and came back to Hazel. I prayed for guidance from the Holy Spirit and my guardian angel.

I waited, expecting to hear some kind of direction. It had been a few days since I left the house, and I knew it was time to head back. There wasn't much I could do with the condition of my feet. I couldn't hike anymore and needed time to recover.

I felt the Great Spirit was pleased with my efforts.

Driving from Echo Lake on Highway 103 toward Idaho Springs, I spotted a gated dirt road that led to the Idaho Springs Cemetery.

Being compelled to rise to the challenge of the test—*just this one last thing to do*—I put I put Hazel in four-wheel drive and drove up the steep rocky road on the mountain side into the cemetery. It was a rough and rocky drive, and I wasn't keen on four-wheeling, but Hazel made it and I pulled to the side.

Pulling out my Pieta prayer book, I prayed for the souls buried here. The cemetery was very old, with headstones from the 1800s. Most of the people buried here died at a young age and there were many children's graves. These early pioneers were to be commended for spirit and tenacity in surviving through the brutal mountain winters. It was very peaceful here and was a lovely way to end my trip as I slowly drove through the cemetery, reading the headstones.

I hadn't intended to stop here and was ready to find food and get back home. Stopping at a convenience store in Idaho Springs, I went inside and bought a Top Ramen cup of noodles soup and a drink. A police officer saw that I was injured and asked if I was okay, and if I needed help. I knew I must have looked as beat as I felt.

There was another BOLO out for me.

I told him I was okay and about to head back home to Denver. He asked if my family knew where I was and I told him, "No, and they were probably worried." Asking my name, he asked me to wait while he checked reports of missing persons.

Sure enough, Thomas was worried. There was another BOLO out for me. After a few minutes, he came back, saying that my husband had called in an alert, and they were sending a message to him to let him know I was okay and on my way home.

Thanking the police officer, I hopped back in Hazel and finished my soup, which had never tasted so delicious. The warm broth was soothing and filling; my last real meal real meal had been the day before at the lodge and I was so grateful for this simple meal.

When I arrived home, Thomas came out and helped me in the house. I told him I would explain everything and tell him where I went, but for now I desperately needed to have a shower and rest. Leaning heavily on his arm he led me back to our bedroom. I was shocked when I saw there had been a fire.

The bedroom walls were scorched.

In the corner of the bedroom, the walls were scorched up to the ceiling. It appeared the fire ignited from a candle on the nightstand. A few photos I had sitting there were little piles of ash. My Bible was untouched. The candle jar was blackened and looked like it had burned intensely. It didn't make sense that it would burn out of control that way.

I asked him, "When did we have the fire and who started it?"

Thomas said he didn't know how it started, this was his first time seeing it. I looked at him in shock. Obviously, I had not been home and Thomas hadn't lit the candle and started the fire.

What had started it?

My joy at being home was short-lived as I wondered at the supernatural forces I had been battling. I had so many questions, but I knew part of winning the Game was not talking about it or asking for help. Fear could not be shown, but I was committed to doing whatever I could to deliver the message … to win.

By learning how to ground myself and channel energy, I was able to stay alive, help heal my body from extreme exposure, meditate and deal with being lost and alone in the woods. A convergence of east meets west.

Yet, I know the path home to salvation was through Jesus Christ.

forty-two
My Final Thoughts

Recovery was an ongoing daily effort for many years.

I am grateful to Grand County Search and Rescue and my family who helped me get through this and didn't give up on finding me.

My hope is that **endurance** will help others to keep from making some of the cardinal mistakes I made.

The US National Parks reported between 2004 and 2014, 46,609 individuals were lost, requiring search and rescue. The statistics aren't good. Usually, after four days, a rescue becomes a recovery of a body.

The good news is that 97% are found within 24 hours and most are found alive.

According to the National Park Service, some 120 to 150 people die each year hiking in the United States. Not surprisingly, day hikers are most at risk because they lack survival skills and rarely plan for an overnight in the mountains.

I was lucky and blessed to survive and feel gratitude that I can share what I have learned in the mountains and help prepare you for the worst-case scenario. I was told by one rescuer, "Every day hiker should be prepared for a worst-case scenario—meaning being stranded overnight."

Recovery was an ongoing daily effort for many years. Living in the middle, between two worlds and realities, was a difficult balance to find. At first, I was overwhelmed and overcome by fear. Gradually I came to feel changed and empowered with my newfound knowledge about life and death. I didn't fear death anymore—the proverbial question about what happens when you die had been answered for me.

No one knew how I was suffering other than Thomas. He lived with it, observed it, and was shocked at some of my actions and reactions from the depth of the mental and physical trauma that had assaulted me. Yet, he only knew a fraction of my experiences and fears. It wasn't until I started my writing that I finally revealed the nightmares that had become my norm.

The effects of PTSD and demons that haunted me were so extreme that it took seven years to get back to where I was healed enough that I could live my life somewhat normally again. I had been so alone.

I have never lost my love of hiking and being in the mountains and nature. They call to me still. When the outdoors call to us, Thomas and I put on our hiking boots, grab the dogs, and head to the trails.

I seriously began the cathartic process of writing this book three years ago. That was a test of **endurance**. After losing my completed book files multiple times, I started over again. I was determined to share my experience and message of love. And Thomas bought me a new computer to complete my mission.

After years of daily prayers including the rosary, and with daily energy self-healing and meditation, the trauma and fear subsided and cleared with faith and remembrance of God's light, love, forgiveness, and promise of eternal life … a promise to the world. I am grateful that God gave me a second chance.

My personal healing has helped me process and cleanse energy that was stuck in my body, mind, and heart and has been key in helping me with physical, emotional, and spiritual healing.

> *For God so loved the world, that He gave his only begotten Son and whosoever believeth in Him shall not perish but have everlasting life.*
> —John 3:16

My Love and Peace to You,
—Kelly Ashford

 **Epilogue**

My memories flooded back as I wrote the final chapters of **endurance**. Questions kept surfacing.

Was the Bad Rental a Bad Seed?

Was the house that seemed to generate bad things, bad vibes, and bad experiences part of what had influenced me in the Game?

When did things start going bad?

When did Thomas and I feel angry all the time with each other?

When did we started fighting with our family and our kids?

When did we all start challenging each other and make accusations that were baseless?

Was the house we rented already inhabited by bad things?

Was it the house … could it have been the house … the house that we had moved into after the mortgage crisis hit, crashing home values? We were upside down and had to reduce our costs, and we had done it fast. We cleared out our 3,700 square-foot home that we loved, donating a truckful of furniture to a women's shelter.

We moved into a smaller place in Denver, grateful to cut our housing costs in half. From the moment we occupied the rental home, unsettling and weird and creepy things began to happen.

Arguments seemed to erupt spontaneously. It felt like there was a presence of some sort within the walls, especially at night. Boomer was attacked in the fenced backyard. We discovered him cowered in the corner; his face had been ripped open, which led to two surgeries. We never knew how it happened.

Paige and Ryan were reporting odd things happening in the game room and in their bedrooms. Paige's bedroom and the game room were both in the basement. There was a narrow stairway; only one person could go up or down at a time. The walls were a dark green. And the hallway had strange fake wood paneling and an overhead light that gave off a green hue that buzzed. She reported that she could hear constant knocking on the walls surrounding her bedroom.

They were awakened by the couch shaking and the TV going static.

She hung sheets from the ceiling to create another visual barrier to make it feel safer from what she thought were the bad walls. When she came in at night and went to the basement, she would race to her bedroom and close the door off from the game room. One time, her boyfriend was over and they fell asleep watching a movie. They were awakened by the couch shaking and the TV going static.

Ryan revealed that things would move around and lights would turn on and off. Coins he left on a table would vanish. And liquids would be poured on his gaming system—all adding more tension within the household. His car was vandalized, along with those of his visiting friends' cars during the night.

Why was all this happening?

As I was finishing this book, Thomas and I visited Paige for a few days. We both looked forward to some time with her. With me were the printed-out chapters. Now an adult on her own, I asked if she would read what I had written and revealed.

She knew I was finally pulling it all together, as did Ryan, who was stationed overseas. I wanted her memories of when I was rescued and brought to the small hospital. She had much to say … far more than I expected. And she disclosed things about what became known as the bad rental house before my lost-in-the-wilderness experience. Paige and Ryan both felt there was something wrong … odd about the house. Paige shared:

I felt uneasy at that house. I always wanted to isolate myself. I felt angry and never wanted to stay and didn't feel welcome.

I wasn't the only one affected; I could tell it affected Tom. He used to be happy go lucky but now it seemed as though he was always angry. I truly believe whatever was going on in that house made him act this way.

I felt that there was a demonic presence. Was there?

I then wondered:

Did that house have anything to do with what happened to me?

Was it a factor in the extreme behavior that overtook me?

Was the house that seemed to generate bad things, bad vibes, and bad experiences play a part in seducing me in the Game?

I now know that the sudden change in my medications could be a factor in some of my behavior changes and moods, as well as poor decisions I made when I was lost. But the unusual experiences felt by my family in the house had nothing to do with my lack of medication or behavior. There was something else.

All of us refer to the rental home as *the bad house.* When we moved away from it ten months after my rescue, it took more than seven years to feel any sense of normalcy had entered my life again.

Flashbacks haunted me. I was unable to articulate what I had experienced. Answers eluded me. I didn't know what to do with my Heaven and Hell near-death experiences. The Voice circulated around, encouraging me to engage in risky behavior. Eventually, it disappeared. I enveloped myself in daily prayer—prayers for light and love to surround me and my family and for forgiveness. And I prayed for what had terrorized me to turn into a Christ light.

I believe to this day that it was my ongoing prayers for light and love that pushed the dark elements away … for me … for my family.

Kelly Ashford

Endurance is the ideal word for Kelly Ashford. A fourteenth-generation Colorado native, her roots are deep with a large extended family. She's hiked several of the acclaimed 14ers in the Rockies—most with her husband Thomas. She has taken the base to the top of Mt. Elbert, Colorado's highest peak, by herself.

Her "lost in the mountain wilderness" over an eleven-day period in June of 2010 became a gripping nightmare for her family, the search team that finally participated after calls from her husband Thomas, and to herself.

On a clear day, the mountains still call to her. Her free time is spent hiking the many nearby hiking trails, enjoying time in nature with her two rescue dogs. A lifelong student, learning is cherished in her household. Her interests include learning about world religions and spirituality, mythology, history, cooking, energy healing and natural remedies, yoga, daily prayer, and meditation.

Her most precious gifts she has are her belief in God and country and the presence of family.

Her story is one of **endurance,** the will to survive, and how prayer and faith kept her alive in June of 2010.

Kelly is the mother of two and relishes the time that she can spend with them, her husband, and Sim and Tula Sue—Indian reservation rescue dogs. She calls Colorado home.

How to work with Kelly

Speaking

Kelly would be delighted to speak about the process of writing her book; her faith; and how she endured and survived being lost in the wilderness.

Book Clubs

Kelly is available to book clubs to talk about **endurance** in-person in Colorado or on Zoom. *Discussion Questions* to consider are included below. All participants must have a copy of the **endurance** book. It can be obtained through online stores, including Amazon and Barnes & Noble. Bookstores can obtain copies for their Book Club members, usually at a discount to them. And signed copies can be received from the author through her website:

KellyAshford.com

Acknowledgments

Resources

Acknowledgments

I would like to express my sincere gratitude to Dr. Judith Briles, The Book Shepard, my Editor.

She helped me so much in writing and transforming the final copy of my book. Judith's belief in my story as one worth telling encouraged me to keep writing about the events that happened in 2010 and inspired me to share my tale of Endurance. I always looked forward to our writing sessions with anticipation of how she would so easily guide me to dig deeper and remember details sometimes forgotten.

Judith has truly made my story better with her creativity and wealth of knowledge and experience she has as a successful editor. I feel blessed to have worked with Judith, an extraordinary Author, Editor, Shepherd, and friend.

I am grateful to Mark Camacho, owner of 81 Media International. Mark was the first professional to lay eyes on my manuscript and through his encouragement and recommendation I was introduced to Dr. Judith Briles who was essential to getting published. As a media specialist and producer, Mark's expressed opinion that **endurance** had a chance for success gave me confidence to pursue the road to publishing with potential of a docu-series or theatrical release.

My sincere gratitude goes to Rebecca Finkel owner of F+P Graphic Design. Rebecca's book cover design and illustrations have made **endurance** even better. Rebecca's expertise and intuition of what would convey to the reader a glimpse of the story has been a key element to a successful final copy of publishing.

To Peggie Ireland and Barb Wilson, final proofreaders. Thank you for catching grammar and punctuation corrections and helping with the flow of my **endurance** story.

List of Supplies for a Day Hike

Most hikes are for just a few hours. But sometimes, a few hours can lead to overnight because of circumstances not under your control, including a change in the weather, injury, even a sudden illness.

It's wise to plan for the unexpected. *If you live alone who is your go-to person if you need assistance?* Start with informing those in your household where you are going and for how long you expect to be away. Let them know.

For ANY hikes, you should have ...

GPS/Satellite/Smartwatch accident alert

Install the Hiker Alert App on your mobile—Shares vital information with your family and friends.

Fully charged phone and solar charger

Flashlight—have extra batteries

Firestarter/Lighter

Waterproof Matches

Sunscreen at least 30spf

Bug Repellant

Water Purifying Bottle

Feminine supplies (may even be used as first aid)

Medications

Compass

Whistle

Mirror

Space blanket

Knife

Nutrition (2 days' worth)

First Aid Kit/Hand Disinfectant

Duct Tape

Raingear

Backpack

Backup Emergency Kit for Car

Mini brush/comb & Hairband

Travel Toothbrush/Toothpaste

Powder Electrolyte Packets

Gallon of Water

Roadside Car Emergency Kit/ LED Road Flares

Socks

Gloves, Wool Stocking Cap

Pants & Long-Sleeved Shirt

Warm Jacket

Blanket & Small Pillow

Sturdy Shoes

Tissue/Toilet Paper, Wet Wipes

Garbage Bags

Reading Material/Trivia Game/
Paper & Pen